One-Week Dungeons

One-Week Dungeons
Diaries of a Seven-Day Roguelike Challenge

David L. Craddock

CRC Press
Taylor & Francis Group
Boca Raton London New York

CRC Press is an imprint of the
Taylor & Francis Group, an **informa** business

First Edition published 2022
by CRC Press
6000 Broken Sound Parkway NW, Suite 300, Boca Raton, FL 33487-2742

and by CRC Press
4 Park Square, Milton Park, Abingdon, Oxon, OX14 4RN

CRC Press is an imprint of Taylor & Francis Group, LLC

Library of Congress Cataloging-in-Publication Data
A catalog record has been requested for this book.

ISBN: 978-1-032-05246-5 (hbk)
ISBN: 978-1-032-05156-7 (pbk)
ISBN: 978-1-003-19672-3 (ebk)

DOI: 10.1201/9781003196723

Typeset in Garamond
by codeMantra

Books by David L. Craddock

Fiction
Arthur and the Knights of the Cafeteria Table (2021)
The Dumpster Club
Heritage: Book One of the Gairden Chronicles
Point of Fate: Book Two of the Gairden Chronicles
Firebug: War of the Elementalists
Nonfiction
Stay Awhile and Listen: Book I – How Two Blizzards Unleashed Diablo and Forged a Video-Game Empire
Stay Awhile and Listen: Book II – Heaven, Hell, and Secret Cow Levels
Arcade Perfect: How Pac-Man, Mortal Kombat, and Other Coin-Op Classics Invaded the Living Room
Monsters in the Dark: The Making of X-COM: UFO Defense
Beneath a Starless Sky: Pillars of Eternity and the Infinity Engine Era of RPGs
Rocket Jump: Quake and the Golden Age of First-Person Shooters
Break Out: How the Apple II Launched the PC Gaming Revolution
Dungeon Hacks: How NetHack, Angband, and Other Roguelikes Changed the Course of Video Games
Shovel Knight (Boss Fight Books)
Bottomless Pit: Bottomless Pit: Running and Jumping Through Platform Games - Volume 1
GameDev Stories: Interviews About Game Development and Culture
GameDev Stories: Volume 2 – More Interviews About Game Development and Culture
Once Upon a Point and Click: The Tale of King's Quest, Gabriel Knight, and the Queens of Adventure Games
One-Week Dungeons: Diaries of a Seven-Day Roguelike Challenge
Making Fun: Stories of Game Development - Volume 1
Angels, Devils, and Boomsticks: The Making of Demons with Shotguns
Anything But Sports: The Making of FTL
Red to Black: The Making of Rogue Legacy

Everybody Shake! The Making of Spaceteam
Stairway to Badass: The Making and Remaking of Doom (TBD 2021)
Ascendant: The Fall of Tomb Raider and the Rise of Lara Croft (TBD 2021)
Bet on Black: How Microsoft and the Xbox Changed Pop Culture (TBD 2022)
Better Together: Stories of EverQuest (TBD)

Contents

7

8

Acknowledgments

To Darren Grey, Bastien Gorissen, Edward Kolis, Joshua Day, Yuji Kosugi, Carles Salas, Ash Monif, Randis Albion, Mark Domowicz, Ido Yehieli, and Joseph Bradshaw. Thank you for sharing your stories with me.

To Mom.

To Amie.

Introduction: Architects
of Permadeath

When developers and players say "role-playing game (RPG)," they're typically talking about a virtual adventure where players control one protagonist or a party of characters, battle monsters, complete quests, increase core attributes such as strength and intellect, and save a world from disaster. That's a broad definition, so players and developers categorize different types of RPGs according to a wide array of subgenres. The action-RPG, popularized by Blizzard North's *Diablo*, emphasizes combat and downplays story and character progression. Massively multiplayer online role-playing games (MMORPGs) support hundreds or thousands of players at once and require an Internet connection to inhabit.

Roguelikes are one of the oldest types of RPGs, and one of the most popular. Created in the late 1970s, roguelike games see players explore procedurally generated dungeons, levels built through algorithms that produce new dungeons every time players sit down to the game. In most roguelikes, characters can only be killed once, a mechanic known as permadeath: upon death, the character is erased, and players start from scratch. Other roguelike trappings include text-based graphics instead of colored 2D or 3D characters and environments; a game structure optimized for a solitary adventurer rather than multiplayer players, like an MMORPG; and turn-based gameplay, where players (traditionally represented by an "@" character) and monsters (represented by capital letters) take turns moving and attacking. As we will soon see, many of these iconic elements are optional.

[Author's Note: Read *Dungeon Hacks: How NetHack, Angband, and Other Roguelikes Changed the Course of Video Games* for a comprehensive overview of early roguelike games.]

Rogue, first released in 1980. Early roguelikes used text instead of color graphics to represent characters and environments. The player, represented by the "@"symbol, approaches the staircase to the next level, represented by the percent "%" sign (Image: Wikipedia).

Don't let the term "roguelike" fool you. *Rogue* was not the first of its kind, but it has been the most influential. Jay Fenlason, an obsessed *Rogue* player motivated to do one better, wrote *Hack*, a larger game sporting new features and items. Robert Koeneke aspired to clone *Rogue* by mixing the game with J.R.R. Tolkien's richly detailed *The Lord of the Rings* lore, which begat *Moria*, which, in turn, led to *Angband*. *Hack* grew into *NetHack*, which indirectly influenced the direction of Thomas Biskup's *Ancient Domains of Mystery* (*ADOM*).

On and on the roguelike genre goes, thanks to a community of developers scattered far and wide across the Internet. Some of them write archetypal dungeon hacks derived from *Rogue*'s timeless pedigree; others produce a new twist on established gameplay by blending mechanics from other types of games, such as shooters and puzzlers, with conventional roguelike systems like procedurally generated levels and permadeath.

That spirit of freewheeling experimentation extends to the 7-day roguelike challenge, or 7DRL. Every year, anyone interested in writing a roguelike is invited to give it a go. The rub: they have only seven consecutive days, blocked out during a weekend-to-weekend period. At the end of 168 hours, the Internet calls "pencils down," and all participants must show their work.

The 2013 7DRL challenge was scheduled to take place from Saturday, March 9th, through Sunday the 17th—right around the time I was neck-deep in research for *Dungeon Hacks*, my book that chronicles the making of and culture surrounding early roguelike games. As I already had roguelike games on the brain, I posted a notice on several popular roguelike forums, asking any developers who planned to participate if they would let me tag along with them in order to document their efforts.[1]

My idea was simple: I would give any interested developers a call on Skype during each day of the challenge, then transcribe the interviews in a series of journal-style logs. Our daily chats would be brief so as to not pose a distraction, and would cover the basics: what they had accomplished that day, what tasks were giving them trouble, what was on the agenda for the next day, and how they were feeling about their progress.

Eleven developers (some working alone, some in teams) responded. Not all of them succeeded.

Before we dig into the meat of the 7DRL challenge, I'd like to talk a bit about how our week-long schedule worked, and how I structured *1-Week Dungeons*.

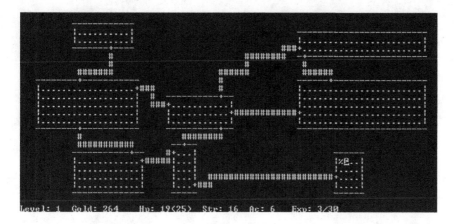

First, I coordinated a regular meeting time with each participant so that I could work around their busy schedules. Each conversation covers ground over one 24-hour period. For instance, Darren Grey chose Sunday, March 10th, as his official start date, so our day-one chat covered Sunday the 10th through Monday the 11th, day two covered Monday the 11th through Tuesday the 12th, and so on.

Second, think of how a disassembled car looks; lots of pieces and parts spread out across a (probably greasy) floor. You know all those pieces and parts do *something* essential, but you would be hard-pressed to explain any particular component's function if asked. Embryonic games can be just as difficult to understand. Therefore, in order to visually document how each 7DRL project evolved as the week progressed, I asked my volunteers to include images from their works in progress throughout the week. Some of them provided more than others. In cases where images were in short supply, I scoured personal blogs and the 7DRL website, 7drl.org, where participants typically post their work.

Third, to avoid chewing through too much of their time on day one, I scheduled a meet-and-greet call ahead of each participant's chosen start date. Those conversations were recorded in the "Day Zero" interviews.

Author

David L. Craddock lives with his wife, Amie Kline-Craddock, in Canton, Ohio. He is the author of several books including *Stay Awhile and Listen: Book I: How Two Blizzards Unleashed Diablo and Forged a Video-Game Empire*, and *Heritage: Book One of the Gairden Chronicles*. Follow David online at davidlcraddock.com, facebook.com/davidlcraddock, and @davidlcraddock on Twitter.

1

Day Zero: Bold Ambitions

Darren Grey

Game: *Mosaic*
Date: Friday, March 8th

Darren Grey is a prominent figure in the roguelike community. He is the co-founder—along with *ASCII Dreams* blogger Andrew Doull—and a co-host of Roguelike Radio, a semi-regular podcast on anything and everything roguish, and a pro of both the genre and the 7DRL challenge. Despite his bonafides, he is affable, is articulate, and shares a common bond with many of his online pals: he died in *Hack*. A lot.

> You go through, and you die, and you play again, and you die, and you play again, and you die. That repetitive play—there was a compelling feeling to it, going all the way back to the start. I didn't get very far in *Hack*. I was never very good at it. After that, I found *ADOM*, and I absolutely fell in love with it. The detail, the atmosphere—for ASCII, it was quite pretty. That really pulled me in.

Grey was content to spend several years exploring Thomas Biskup's wonderland. After finishing *ADOM (Ancient Domains of Mystery)* several times, he went online in search of similar games. The trail led him to the 7DRL. "The first roguelike I made, *Gruesome*, was finished a few days before my first 7DRL challenge," Grey recalls.

> I knew that if I made the game, I would have the knowledge I needed to participate. As it happens, I failed the first time I did the challenge. But from the earliest stage of me developing roguelikes, I had my eye on the challenge.

DOI: 10.1201/9781003196723-1

For Grey, the experience of writing code during the 7DRL is as important as the games he invents.

> Now, normally, I have a very busy life, and I don't get nearly as much time to sit down and code as I'd like—partly because one does tend to procrastinate. So it's nice to have this concentrated period of time to say, 'I *must* make a roguelike this week. I have no choice. I will sit down and I will do it, and the rest of my life can go to hell because this is what the week is for.

When I ask Grey to choose a favorite from the 7DRL games he has submitted over the years, he has an answer at the ready.

> *Broken Bottle* was my attempt to do what you may call 'games as art.'[2] I had a lot of ideas in the back of my head about it, and those came out during the week. It was a game about an alcoholic in a post-apocalyptic world. You start off as a happy, content drunk. As you explore, you have choices about whether to continue drinking or not. Those [choices] affect your gameplay in various ways.

Written during the 2011 7DRL, *Broken Bottle* was unique for more than its twist on conventional roguelike mechanics. Grey set out to tell a story, a feat not many roguelike authors attempt due to the procedural generation inherent in the genre.

> I really enjoyed doing those pieces of writings. People reacted very positively. It's the first roguelike that's ever shown all the description in the game in first-person: 'I missed the bandit' and 'The rat hit me.' Writing is another passion of mine, so this game was a chance to explore both passions: a story with bits of text merged with the gameplay.

He received high marks for his efforts: fourth place in the challenge and an in-depth analysis led by Jeff Lait, a staple of the roguelike and 7DRL societies and an idol of Grey's. Even so, Grey did not let the commendations go to his head. The journey of 7DRL, not the destination, was the ultimate reward. "In such a short span of time, you experience such a whirlwind of emotions. There's nothing else like it. It's my favorite week of the year."

Although Grey expresses enthusiasm for the approaching 2013 7DRL, his week outside of game development is full. He is in the middle of a critical project at work and will have to work several late nights during the challenge—something with which Grey has some experience. During his first 7DRL, he juggled two full-time jobs and a relationship. "Definitely exhausted, but satisfied," Grey responds when I ask how he felt at the end of that week. "I don't know of any comparable feeling." He pauses; then, in a testament to his passion for the challenge, adds, "Well, I suppose a comparable feeling might be doing something physically exerting, and then feeling immensely satisfied at the end of it. No specifics, mind," he finished with a laugh.

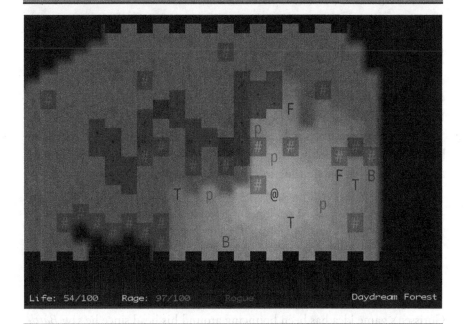

Darren Gray's *Rogue Rage*, an ambitious design he failed to complete for a previous 7-day roguelike challenge.

Life: 54/100   Rage: 97/100   Rogue   Daydream Forest

Grey is raising the bar for 2013. With his next game, *Mosaic*, he aims to take another crack at games-as-art design. Though he intends to start from scratch in terms of writing code, he has a clear vision for how he wants *Mosaic* to play out. Controlling an "@" avatar, players will move across maps consisting of blank tiles. Every time they pass over a tile, its color will change.

> If you keep going over them in certain patterns, you'll build wall tiles. If you manage to make an enclosure of wall tiles—four sides that make up a square, three sides that make up a triangle, something like that— they'll fill in automatically with a range of mosaic tiles.

Enemies—represented by capital letters—appear in each level and roam the map, smashing through tiles and disrupting the player's designs. *Mosaic* will eschew traditional bump-based combat. The only way to defeat enemies is to pen them inside colored squares.

To maximize coding time, he'll be coding *Mosaic* using the T-engine, a construct design written in the Lua language and pre-loaded with routines written specifically for roguelike games. "Reuse everything you can get your hands on," Grey suggests.

> It [7DRL challenge] is about making a game, not building an engine. Things like FOV [field of view] code should absolutely be reused. Find a good, existing dungeon generator. It's about finding the right pieces to put together so you've got something unique at the end.

Bastien Gorissen

Game: *BattleRL*

Date: Saturday, March 9th

Bastien Gorissen has played relatively few roguelikes, but he fell head over heels for the genre quickly. After playing hours of *Dwarf Fortress*, he decided to try his hand at contributing to his new favorite type of game.

> I wanted to take part [in the 7DRL challenge] last year, but didn't have the time. I think I need deadlines to get a roguelike done. I have played around with the idea for I don't know how many years, but I know that if I [set a deadline] of 'when it's done,' I'll get lost in creating levels. I'll spend forever on them and never go beyond that. So I like the idea of saying to myself, 'I have one week. I must finish something. I must do everything and have a playable game.'

Gorissen's game idea has been bouncing around his head since he saw *Battle Royale*, a Japanese film based on the novel of the same name, and sharing themes with U.S. author Suzanne Collins's *Hunger Games* trilogy. In *Battle Royale*, teens battle to the death on an abandoned island. At set intervals, sections of the island are partitioned off, herding the survivors closer together for maximum bloodshed.

Fifty teenagers square off in *Battle Royale*. For his game, titled *BattleRL*, Gorissen wants to trim the number of rivals down to 20. Like the film that inspired it, *BattleRL* will unfold on an island that contains ruined buildings and secret caches of weapons. Aggression will go a long way in determining the player's odds of survival against the computer-controlled opponents.

> There are a couple of other rules. The world will shrink; you'll lose access to parts of the world as time goes on, and you only have a certain amount of time to kill everyone else or let them kill each other. That's the basic idea. We'll see how much I can fit within the week [time limit].

Interested in how a first-timer might approach roguelike systems that veterans consider old hat, I ask Gorissen how he plans to tackle map generation, the beating heart of most roguelikes.

> It will be a single-level game, so I'll just generate some kind of island because that's the easiest thing to do. As for the size, I think it will depend on the combat and the A.I. I will see what's interesting for gameplay. If the island is too big, you'll never find anyone, and that's not interesting. But if it's too small, the game will end in 10 minutes. So we'll need to see what's good.

Before we sign off, I ask what tomorrow has in store. "I think I'll start with simple level generation. That will be the first thing I'll do, but I have no idea yet how I'll do that," he admits. Gorissen does not sound nervous, explaining that he downloaded a library of roguelike-centric routines called libtcod to get him up to speed.[7]

Just in case hurdles like map generation prove harder to jump than he thinks, Gorissen wants to finish a few days early so he has plenty of time to tinker.

> I hope to get one item done per day. Tomorrow will probably only be world generation, but I want to move fairly quickly so I can have one or two days at the end just for balancing and polishing; no adding new features.

Edward Kolis

Game: *TriQuest*
Date: Friday, March 8th

"I'm guessing it was a forbidden-fruit thing," Kolis recalls when I ask what led to his fascination with roguelikes.

> My dad had a disk with all these games on it. This was back in the early '90s, so I was about eight years old. He had one of those PCs with a turbo switch and it ran at maybe 12 megahertz. One of the games on this floppy disk was a *Space Invaders* clone, and the other was *NetHack*.

Kolis was allowed to play computer games provided he followed his father's golden rule: do not install games on the hard drive, which had very limited storage space. To his credit, Kolis tried to make do with running *NetHack* directly from the floppy, but the game performed slowly. Hoping his father wouldn't notice, Kolis ran the install program and gleefully recommended his dungeon crawling.

I loved it. It was unlike any other game I'd played: it was so open-ended. Other games gave you very simple things to do: move your spaceship left or right and shoot aliens. But *NetHack* was one of the more detailed games, and I've always been into that kind of game. So has my dad, although he never got into *NetHack*.

> **Decimation** is an early roguelike of Kolis's written for a 7-day roguelike event.

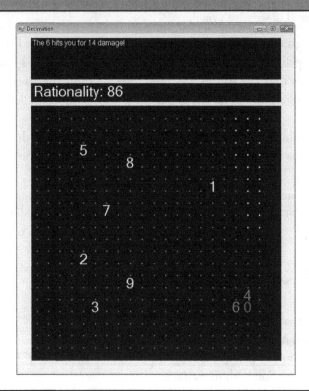

For 2013, he wants to attempt a roguelike design he claims has not been implemented successfully before.

> This one is called *TriQuest*. It's got the number three in it again, but this time you have three heroes. There have been party-based roguelikes, but the ones I've seen had you control one character and the others were controlled by the A.I. [artificial intelligence], or you could switch to another character. My game will have a slightly different mechanic: instead of all three characters occupying separate tiles, they're all in the same tile—but each tile has a 3-by-3 grid, so they're tiles within tiles.

TriQuest's three player-characters follow easily understood archetypes: warrior, mage, and priest. The warrior hacks and slashes, the mage casts spells, and the priest heals his party. By pressing the arrow keys, players will move their party as a cohesive unit. Tapping keys on the number pad rearranges the party's formation, so players can, for instance, tuck the mage away in the back and let the warrior absorb damage up front. To keep adventurers from growing complacent, Kolis plans to give monsters the ability to group in formations and attack the party from different angles.

Traditionally, roguelikes grow more challenging as players descend deeper into their dungeons. For *TriQuest*, Kolis will shun dungeons and craft a sprawling wilderness, much like Arcadia in *ADOM*. "I was thinking of making a gradient map. Take a huge map, kind of like *Legend of Zelda* over-worlds, and place hotspots on it signifying danger." Players would evaluate whether to enter a region based on its terrain. Grasslands would hold easier battles than deserts, which would prove less challenging than wastelands, and so on.

Kolis decided on the C# (pronounced "C Sharp") language for 2013's event. "It's my favorite language. I think it's clean, powerful, and has a lot of libraries behind it. It's maybe not as clean as Python, but I'm familiar with it because I've used it a lot."

Like other 7DRL veterans, Kolis is giddy over the prospect of venturing off the beaten path of the standard dungeon hack. "If I don't do that, I'm just reinventing what's been done before, so what's the point?"

Joshua Day

Game: *Currently Unnamed*
Date: Friday, March 8th

Joshua Day has dabbled in games all his life. In fact, one of his earliest games featured levels composed of text characters, which players navigated by controlling a smiley-face ASCII avatar—the same symbol used to represent the player-character in the PC version of *Rogue*.

It comes as no surprise, then, that Day is drawn to roguelike development. As a lifelong game maker and player, he appreciates the genre's ability to boil visualization down to abstract elements, placing the emphasis squarely on gameplay over graphics. However, he believes the genre can do better.

For 2013, Day wants to improve on the area where he feels roguelikes are most lacking.

> I don't think this mode of interface and style of design is perfect for dungeon crawling. In a sense, the dungeon setting was designed for tabletop play. While it's relatively easy to simulate on a computer, there's so much potential for what we can do, and if we don't tap into that, it's

somewhat of a waste. That being said, this year I'm planning on doing something set in a cave system, so I'm going back to the genre's roots.

Day's game, which he believes will be his magnum opus, will comprise a mix of roguelike elements and puzzles. Indeed, puzzles will factor heavily into the nucleus of his as-yet-unnamed game: along with building dungeons on the fly, Day hopes to procedurally generate puzzles as well.

> Space is incredibly important, so having puzzles where, say, you're trying to push around a group of blocks that are attached to each other, pushing in such a way that two colored blocks line up with each other to open a door you can pass through. That kind of thing.

Day says the game will be more *Rogue* than *Myst*, however. Although every level will throw a variety of conundrums at players, they will have to contend with other threats while they evaluate their surroundings for solutions. Monsters wander the caverns, and players will need to dispatch them in order to poke around in peace. Monsters can also be used to spring mechanisms needed to progress. Day posits a scenario he believes will be possible in the finished game. A corridor contains a pressure plate at one end and a door far, far down at the other end; players would be unable to sprint from the plate to the door in time, but camping out near the door and luring a monster onto the plate would do the trick.

Rook, one of Joshua Day's roguelikes made for a previous challenge.

Day seems confident he can tie together such an ambitious collection of systems in a week—unless a confluence of real-life events transpires against him. When we spoke, Day was waiting to hear back about a job he applied for, and preparing for an overnight stay in New York City with his wife.

> The good news—which is bad news in every other way—is the particular house we were looking at fell through, so we won't be able to get it, so that time is saved. And my job is delayed by another couple of weeks, so I have full days to work on this. The trip to New York is in the middle of the week. Probably an afternoon and the next morning will be gone from that, but I have the whole train ride to think about [my game].

He already has one strike against him. Day tells me he had planned to collaborate on the game with David Ploog, lead designer of the popular *Dungeon Crawl Stone Soup* roguelike, but personal issues had caused Ploog to pull out. Day will be writing the game on his own.

Wisely, he is planning for the worst-case scenario. "I get drawn to ambitious games," he confesses. "The difference here is I think I can get most of it written on the first day, or maybe the first two days." Priority number one, he says, is hatching maps and getting a player-character moving around on the screen. Next is field of view. After that, he'll move on to puzzles.

"The strategy is definitely to get something up and running, something playable and fun, if I'm lucky, and then iterate on that from the very beginning."

Yuji Kosugi and Carles Salas

Game: *Versus Time*
Date: Saturday, March 9th

Seven-day roguelike veterans shared tips and suggestions in a tone equal parts conviction and anticipation for the week ahead. For them, they are lessons learned and proven over years of 7DRL victories and defeats. For Yuji Kosugi, they are lessons to be learned. "I want to make things as simple as possible because this is my first 7DRL. I haven't even shipped a game yet."

Kosugi was introduced to roguelike games through *NetHack*. While in high school, he got a copy of the Debian operating system, which included a repository of free games to download. *NetHack* and *Angband* were on the list. He gave them a go but was unable to decipher all the strange symbols and stats covering his screen.

Nonetheless, he was intrigued. He continued bumbling through dungeons and tried to convince his friends to play, hoping they could learn together. When his new hobby failed to catch on, Kosugi drifted from roguelikes for several years. In 2012, he checked in and discovered a fresh crop of games to play and mysteries to unravel. "I started playing some of the modern rogue-like games. I'm most interested in games in terms of these groups of systems that have interesting interactions, and that give you complicated decisions to make. Roguelikes are pretty much exactly that."

As the 2013 7DRL approached, Kosugi took the plunge and entered the challenge. He will not be working alone. "I discovered the challenge through Yuji [Kosugi] and some people he knows," Carles Salas, Kosugi's partner for the challenge, tells me.

> I haven't played a lot of roguelikes. I think the first ones I played were on the iPhone. I played *100 Rogues* and *Sword of Fargoal* [iOS version], and I just liked them. Slowly, I grabbed a few other games. It's been a very slow-cooking thing for me.

Kosugi and Salas bumped into each other at a game design meet-up in London. Every 2 weeks, programmers, artists, and other amateur developers interested in games organize to get feedback on their projects. In addition to serving as a support system, the meet-up gives budding developers the opportunity to form partnerships if and when their objectives align. Salas, who has a background in graphic design, was intrigued by the game design Kosugi was brainstorming for the challenge and offered to team up.

Kosugi briefly contemplated building a real-time roguelike for two or more players, but dismissed it. Such a feat fell too far outside the scope of the 7-day challenge. The problem was that he could not suss out a way to make a competitive *turn-based* roguelike work either. Games such as *NetHack* and *Angband* allowed players to perform one action per turn. It would take hours for players scattered to all four corners of the dungeon to reach one another.

Then a friend on Twitter posted a video of two professionals playing a match of fast chess, also known as blitz chess. Normal chess gives each player between 60 and 180 minutes to take their turns. Blitz chess grants only 10 minutes per player. The resulting blur of moves can give even the most knowledgeable chess player whiplash, but it gave Kosugi a flash of inspiration.

> I used to play stuff like that, and when I saw it, I thought, That would actually work perfectly. It's like a roguelike, but you have multiple players, and each player can move around and kill monsters and each other, but there's also a clock forcing them to make moves quickly. That might actually work as a competitive, multiplayer game. I guess what we're going to do this week is try to prove that that's true.

Apropos of his motivations, Kosugi christened his 7DRL game *Versus Time*.

Although Salas has experience designing art and interfaces, he, like Kosugi, is a novice at building roguelikes. Both men set a series of modest goals that they can expand on if they still have time left on the clock. "Basically, I want a simple dungeon that fits on the screen. Everybody's in there at the same time. People take turns," Kosugi says.

> There will be some amount of loot and skills for people to pick up and use. Otherwise, [players will be] killing creatures for experience, and, when people feel ready, they can move on to the next level. Once everybody has done that, you move on.

Kosugi and Salas went over their schedules for the week with me. Kosugi works a day job, but plans to request a day off before the weekend to code as much as possible. Salas recently mailed off a treatment for a sitcom to the BBC and is waiting for a yay or nay, leaving his week wide open. In addition to creating artwork, he will put each new build (version) of the game through its pieces and share his thoughts with Kosugi.

> Just from seeing the work he's done on the iOS game he's making, and a card game he's been working on, I knew it would be good to have his opinion on design, and for tweaking the balance on creatures and so on. I asked him to be more closely involved, Kosugi says.

As our day-zero conversation comes to a close, I ask Kosugi what is on tap for day one of *Versus Time* development.

> The key thing will be to get input for multiple players going so that they can move sequentially. Basic things like the timer, and monsters and combat. I'm hoping [monsters and combat] will be straightforward. Once that's done, I want to put in a basic progression system and some skills.

He laughs. "When I describe it that way, it sounds straightforward, but I'm sure there will be complications."

Grimm Bros. (Ash Monif, Randis Albion, Mark Domowicz)

Game: *Dungeon X: Flesh Wounds*
Date: Friday, March 8th

Most 7DRL developers view the annual 168-hour game jam as a one-and-done sprint. Produce a game built around a singular idea, then leave it behind and move on to other projects once the clock expires. Ash Monif and Randis Albion see 2013's challenge as a launch pad for something bigger.

"Randis [Albion] and I are long-time collaborators," Monif tells me during our conference call.

> We worked with each other on multiple projects over the years and have been in the industry for over 10 years each. We worked on a multitude of titles—everything from big, triple-A titles to small, indie titles. We felt it was time to offer gamers a different kind of choice in their gaming.

Shortly after forming their company, Grimm Bros., LLC, Monif and Albion decided to design a roguelike or at least a game with roguelike elements—referred to within the industry as a roguelike-like. They hired Mark Domowicz as one of their first programmers. Whereas Monif and Albion have little experience playing roguelikes, Domowicz has been playing them for 4 years. He discovered *NetHack* while working on a role-playing game (RPG) at a previous job.

Domowicz's curiosity led him to code several prototype roguelikes, one of which comprises the base for Grimm Bros.'s entry in the 2013 7DRL—*Dungeon X: Flesh Wounds.*

> We're working on our first project and have been developing it for a little while, now. We're entering the 7DRL in order to accelerate it. We're going into a sprint and hope to come out with a playable demo of an early iteration of what the final game will be. We're thrilled to be joining the 7DRL community, Monif says.
>
>   *[Author's Note: The Grimm Bros. team consisted of more*
>   *than Monif, Albion, and Domowicz when we spoke,*
>   *but only those three took part in our daily chats.]*

The Grimm Bros. team holds no illusions that *Dungeon X* will be feature-complete at the end of 7 days. In fact, it might not even be called *Dungeon X* by the time the guys are ready to release it to market. "This will be an early preview where you get an introduction to maybe one or two of our characters, some of the monsters, some of the mechanics, and the look and feel of our world," Monif explains.

For the next 7 days, Monif, Albion, and Domowicz all want to place equal emphasis on their game's look and feel. Big on levity, the trio sends me concept art depicting a vibrant, storybook-esque world inhabited by characters and creatures straight out of a fairy tale. When I express as much, the guys enthusiastically explain that that is their intention: the lead character, a slight blonde in a familiar-looking red cloak, resembles a slightly older Little Red Riding Hood.

The three Grimm Bros. developers outline the roles they will play over the following week. Domowicz, as the programmer, will concentrate on building on top of one of his early prototype games. Albion will function as a one-man art studio, turning out concept art and in-game models for characters and levels.

Monif will "take point," as he put it, as the producer—a cheerleader who will aim to keep the guys energized and coordinate tasks. "We are going to start full-bore on Sunday, so midnight tonight. We're going to have one more planning meeting, and then we're going to go full throttle on this. We'll be done next Sunday," Monif asserts.

"We're not doing it for crazy fame and exposure," Albion says.

> We're doing it because we like doing it. It's something we want to prove to ourselves: that we can do this in seven days. We have experience in this field, so we want to see how far we can go in seven days.

Ido Yehieli

Game: *Fisticuffsmanship*
Date: Friday, March 8th

Like many roguelike designers, Ido Yehieli favors function over form. A veteran of the 7DRL challenge since 2008, he points to *Fuel*, his 2012 game, as his favorite entry thus far.[3] He got the idea for the game, a 2D platformer-roguelike hybrid, after playing *Spelunky*, a game in the same vein but, according to Yehieli, not as heavy on roguelike mechanics as he would have liked.

> *Fuel* is turn-based, grid-based, and everything is discrete. It's a rogue-like, but you view it from the side, and gravity plays a role. You really have to be careful about where you're heading and not falling from ledges. It's got depth that you don't get from a top-down [view] game, which is quite dangerous. I'm quite proud of it.

For his next game, Yehieli wants to challenge players to attack enemies in new ways. "In a lot of roguelikes, there's interesting stuff on a higher tactical level: what kind of special actions can I take? What kind of spells can I cast? Should I use this potion? Should I not use it?" he explains.

> But the mechanics of most roguelikes boils down to walking around and bumping into enemies to attack them. That's pretty boring. I want to make it interesting by making your ability to attack and to defend yourself a combination of your surroundings—how sheltered you are, such as whether there are walls on all sides or you're out in the open.

Yehieli's idea, *Fisticuffsmanship*, will strip away all the established RPG attributes and leave only two—attack and defense. Various sets of circumstances will enhance or attenuate the player's attack and defense values. For example, players with their backs up against a wall will receive a boost to defense. Walking in the same direction over concurrent turns is tantamount to a forward charge, causing the game to increase the player's attack rating.

Yehieli cautions that those scenarios are hypothetical for now. His goal is for players to carefully examine each level and base movement on their proximity to architecture that will give them advantages against enemies.

> One thing I have thought about that I'm not sure will work is to have the color of your character represent your status. You have stats for attack and defense, as well as how many hit points you've got. When you represent color with HTML, you're working with RGB [red, green, and blue] values. So your health will determine how high your red value is, your defense affects how high your green value is, and your attack affects your blue value.

To write *Fisticuffs*, Yehieli will interlace HTML and JavaScript so that players can run the game directly from the web browser of their choice. Tonight, he'll continue building the game's skeleton—just enough so he can get right to work basic input/output mechanisms like player movement working tomorrow, his first official day of 7DRL coding.

> In previous years, especially the last two years, I really focused on aesthetics. I had fully-animated graphics and nice music. This year I'm not focusing on that at all. I'm making a pure ASCII game to focus purely on gameplay. This is a game about timing your moves to those of your enemies, and I have a couple of mechanics that I really want to get in.

As for bells and whistles, Yehieli is content to let his programming muse guide him. "It's not just hard to plan—it's also less fun. I don't like to start coding with a full blueprint. It's more fun to mix in creativity throughout the development cycle."

Joseph Bradshaw

Game: *KlingonRL*
Date: Saturday, March 9th

Joseph Bradshaw tossed his name in the 7DRL hat for reasons quite different than those of his peers. Like many, he stumbled across a *Hack* disk, died repeatedly, but was intrigued enough to press on. He printed out a lengthy strategy guide to the game and kept it close at hand, referencing it when an unfamiliar ASCII character reared its head.

A few years later, Bradshaw entered his first 7DRL, and that's where his story strays from the beaten path.

> What happened was I got really ill. Right around 2009, I became too ill to do much. I spent a lot of time on the Internet and found the Rogue Temple, which is where I saw your post about you doing your book. I'd been lurking on that forum. I did a little bit of computer science in college, so people occasionally had programming questions I could help them with.

All the while, Bradshaw's health deteriorated. Following a perfunctory exam, his doctor diagnosed him with sleep apnea and outfitted him with a continuous positive airway pressure (CPAP) machine—which Bradshaw describes as "one of those Darth Vader masks"—to clear his airway at night.

Rather than help, the machine exacerbated his infections. He slept for 20 hours at a time but woke up feeling as if he'd napped for a few minutes. Over time, his ragged breathing wreaked havoc on his organs. "You have heart problems, liver problems, and you can't focus. Obviously you can't focus," he explained.

> You have all kinds of cognitive issues. It got to the point where I was having minor heart attacks. I'd fall over and pass out in the store. Not fully [losing consciousness], but thinking, *Oh, fuck. Here I go. I'm having an attack.*

Another trip to the doctor, another solution: steroids. Bradshaw took them as prescribed and ballooned from 215 pounds to 280. The next step was for Bradshaw to go under the knife. When he came back up, the breathing problems persisted.

> After the last surgery I had, I wasn't feeling better. My doctor said, 'Well, the surgery was successful.' I asked how she defined success because I was still really sick, ...What was really upsetting was she was telling me I couldn't breathe because I was fat. I came to her at 215 pounds. All the steroids and years of drugs, and I went up to 280. I came to her not being able to breathe, and I was really thin. Now I'm super fat and still can't breathe.

During a visit with a friend, Bradshaw hit on the source of his troubles. After years of respiratory issues purportedly related to asthma, his friend underwent allergy tests and found that she was allergic to eggs and dairy. She eliminated them from her diet and bounced back almost overnight.

Bradshaw was willing to try anything. Before 2009, he had been a successful attorney. Since getting sick, he had had to leave his job and move back home with his parents. After conferring with his friend, he took an allergy test and finally got some answers. Dairy and wheat were allergens bombs that had ripped through his insides.

> I'd been sick for so many years, and no doctor had ever been like, 'Hey, maybe it's something in your diet. Let's check your diet out.' They were condescending and shitty to me: 'Oh, maybe it's all in your head.' Yeah. That's why my face is bleeding. I would bleed out of my nose and mouth. I was going blind in one of my eyes because the pressure inside was out of control.

Bradshaw eliminated wheat and dairy from his diet and bounced back—not as quickly as his friend, but fast enough to tackle the 2013 7DRL with alacrity.

> I'm calling it *KlingonRL* right now, and I'll probably stick with the *Star Trek* theme, even though I went with it last year. I've always wanted to make this game; it's the one I wanted to make last year until I realized I didn't have the energy to do it.

To win, players must navigate through star systems, breach Federation space, and destroy the Genesis device—a terraforming procedure that played a central role in *Star Trek II: The Wrath of Khan*—while managing their ammo, fuel, and hull plating. Instead of presenting players with a victory screen upon destroying the device, *KlingonRL* will require them to fly all the way back to their Klingon home system with Federation ships—including the famous Enterprise—in hot pursuit.

All interactions will take place using the roguelike genre's classic *bump* system. "Bumping is the essential thing that happens in roguelike control schemes," Bradshaw reasons.

> In *Super Mario Bros.* and other platformers, jumping is the thing. Jumping hits blocks, jumping smashes enemies; it's how you find goodies and secrets, and it's how you traverse terrain. In *Rogue* and roguelikes, it's about bumping [into enemies and items to initiate actions].

In *KlingonRL*, each bump triggers a contextual reaction. Bumping gas giants top off fuel, bumping a Federation cruiser blows it up, bumping planets beam up radioactive isotopes to refill ammo, and bumping Klingon star bases patch up and refuel the ship.

At the outset of the game, players will hold the element of surprise. Their Klingon vessel starts cloaked. Enemy ships patrol erratically, oblivious to players. But the moment players bump an object, their cloak dissipates and nearby vessels converge on their position. If players can survive for a handful of turns, the cloak restores, and enemies will drift away.

For my final question, I ask Bradshaw what language he will be using to write the game. I've posed this question to all the developers because I enjoy seeing how developers apply different languages and toolsets to the same general challenge. Bradshaw's toolset of choice: *GameMaker*, a robust application that enables users to create games through a combination of writing code and dragging and dropping elements.

By the end of our hour-long call, Bradshaw sounds just as alert and excited as when our conversation began.

> I just got better over the last couple of months. You're actually talking to me during a very interesting time. I've been down for years. Now I'm back up and don't know what to do with my life. Making roguelikes is something I did as a child. Now that I'm better, and I'm still making them, I don't know what changes are in store for me as I go back to work and re-engage in professional life.

2

Day One: Programming Benders

Darren Grey

Game: *Mosaic*

Date: Sunday, March 10th—Monday, March 11th

Grey knows he is running a marathon, not a sprint. His goal for day one is modest: assemble a protean game, then add features each day in order to fulfill his vision by 6:00 P.M. the following Sunday, exactly 168 hours from the time he started. By the time we convene on Skype, Grey has been at it for 5 hours and intends to push ahead for a few more after we wrap.

He spent the first half of day one getting organized: installing the T-engine, downloading updates, scrapping routines *Mosaic* would not need to function, copy-and-pasting lines of code from his previous 7DRL games that might come in handy. He lost a bit of time rooting around the Internet to replace a file he deleted, believing *Mosaic* would work just fine without it, only to realize he needed it after all. A typical first day of any 7DRL challenge, he assures me.

His "@" avatar is able to move around the grid of tiles that stretch across his screen. At the start of each game, all the tiles are colored gray. Every time he guides the avatar over a tile, it changes color: to black, to red, to green, and back to the beginning of the cycle. On the one hand, the basic idea, changing the color of tiles by walking over them, seems to be working. On the other hand, the grid is not as vibrant as Grey would like.

"I was trying to get the red tiles to turn into green tiles. I tried 50 different methods and they didn't work."

DOI: 10.1201/9781003196723-2

He spent some time fiddling, then logged into an Internet Relay Chat (IRC) channel to pick the brains of other programmers participating in the challenge. They dispensed some tricks that helped Grey break down the obstruction in his path. "I've had a bit too much chocolate and tea today. It's made me a bit hyper. Not everything's going as smoothly as I wanted so far, but finally, a few things are working."

When I ask what lay ahead for the rest of the night, Gray seems at a loss for a split second. He has to get up for work early tomorrow, and foresees a long day at the office. Before then, he wants to continue building on his foundation. He has hard-coded—programmer jargon for baking in data rather than assigning it to variables, which can be changed as the programmer runs—green and red colors into his engine. That will not do for the final game, he acknowledges; he will need to write code that enables the T-engine to choose from one of dozens, hundreds, or thousands of colors to diversify the titular mosaic-like grid to the greatest degree possible.

"I want to do one thing at a time," Grey declares, maintaining that he does not want to think too far ahead and lose track of the work still on his plate. "Probably sequences, and then filling in rectangles of color, and then looking at getting some enemies in."

Bastien Gorissen

Game: *BattleRL*
Date: Sunday, March 10th—Monday, March 11th
Gorissen wanted to have a map on his screen by the end of day one. He has succeeded, though he is less than thrilled with the results.

> I wanted to generate island-shaped maps. Right now, they're a bit too blocky. The island takes up almost all the map; I want jagged edges around the map. It's not as good as I wanted, but other than that, everything I tried to do worked.

Still, he concedes, the map works. It resembles an island, and that was part of the process he worried would give him the most trouble. "Even if the map isn't [exactly what I want], it's okay as long as the game is fun. Hopefully I'll have a bit of time to go back and do some cool stuff with the map."

To generate terrain, Gorissen applied the Perlin Noise function. Perlin Noise is an algorithm designed by NYU computer science professor Ken Perlin. He created the algorithm as a way to create computer graphics that look more natural than blocky, machine-created graphs and architecture.

Gorissen begins designing *BattleRL*'s playfield.

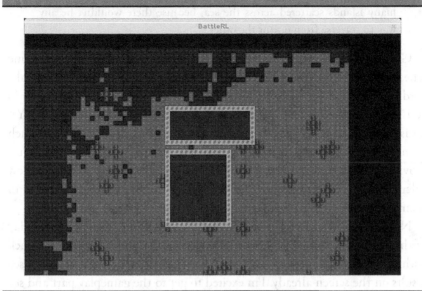

Graphics programmers and researchers frequently call on the algorithm to generate smooth-looking wood, stone, ocean waves, and other textures.

The massive size of Gorissen's map likely led to its blocky composition.

BattleRL, day one. Green (lighter gray) tiles denote wilderness, while Gorissen uses blue (darker gray) to mark off the water surrounding the island where the game takes place. The outlined, box-shaped structures are buildings.

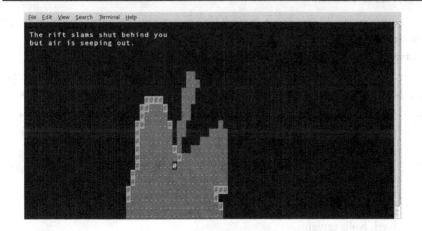

I'm going with a 500-by-500 map. I had to tweak some of the numbers in the generation algorithm so I have one big chunk of land and not many islands scattered across the sea, because there wouldn't be any way to traverse from one or the other.

Gorissen admits that he has yet to settle on *BattleRL*'s look. Since his game relies so heavily on time—sections of the island close off at set intervals, herding players closer together for maximum bloodshed—he would like to add small touches to help players distinguish between day and night. Yet he is wary to dive too deeply into such extraneous details with so much foundational work still in front of him. He has yet to get his "@" avatar moving around, and the presence of characters will necessitate field-of-view calculations to determine how far characters can see around obstacles in their path.

None of that concerns Gorissen. After all, this is only his first official day of the challenge, and he has a few hours left in the tank. "I'm still on track with what I had planned, so I'm feeling pretty good, actually. It's great to see results on the screen already. I'm excited to get to the gameplay part and see how that comes together."

What does concern Gorissen, however, is that he has reached the end of the weekend. Tomorrow, he goes back to his day job. Fortunately, he has planned ahead. He will wake up earlier and code for an hour or two each morning. During his hour-long lunch break, he'll code at his desk while he eats. Fortuitously, he has his evenings free: his girlfriend booked a trip out of town during the challenge, leaving him all evening, every evening to code.

Edward Kolis

Game: *TriQuest*
Date: Saturday, March 9th—Sunday, March 10th

So far, so good—that sums up Kolis's view of his work on *TriQuest* thus far. Map generation was the only item on his schedule for day one. Upon starting a session, the game scatters clusters of numbers 1–10 across the map, which is comprised of a large grid made up of cells. Those seeds determine the danger level of different areas.

You go a certain number of cells out, and a [danger level of] 5 degrades to a 4, then a 4 degrades to a 3, and so on, until you're back down to 1. It's almost like a height map, except not actually height, but danger level, Kolis explains.

Once the routine finishes scattering numbers far and wide, another routine assigns terrain based those numbers. Cells seeded with 1s are grasslands, while 5s are wastelands, the deadliest areas. Forests, lakes, and deserts fall in between grasslands and wastelands.

The whole process of writing the routines and getting a map on the screen took Kolis less than an hour. "I'm thinking that was the easy part. The hard part's coming."

Kolis speaks from experience. Around age 10, Kolis's uncle gave him a copy of *Visual Basic 1.0* for the Windows 3.1 operating system. After very little dabbling, he wrote a clone of *Yahtzee*. In 2008, he applied his programming skills to the 7DRL challenge. His goal was to create a simplified version of *Battalion Wars*, a combat game for Nintendo's Wii console where players fight on foot but can also commandeer tanks. Kolis worked for a couple of days before abandoning the game as too complex.

Determined to succeed, Kolis kept things simple for the 2009 7DRL. He devised a math-oriented game called *Decimation* where, instead of an "@," players controlled a zero (0) and defeated enemies using arithmetic.[4]

> The way you do that is you walk up to them and press '+,' and that adds 3, and it can wrap around [to 0]. You change all the numbers around you using different mathematical operations. It's more of a puzzle-roguelike, I guess you could say. I was successful with that one.

TriQuest, day one. Kolis's map is helter-skelter, with forest, water, and rocky terrain scattered in all directions.

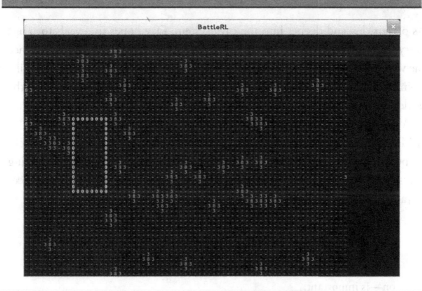

Kolis knows that wish lists can spiral out of control. To stay organized, he jotted down a to-do list for each day of the week. First up: procedural map generation, the heart and soul of any roguelike. "I'm trying to pace myself. If I don't, I won't be able to tell if I've made an appropriate amount of progress one day, or I might get stuck somewhere."

Joshua Day

Game: *Cogs of Cronus*
Date: Sunday, March 10th—Monday, March 11th

To aid him in visualizing how the pieces and parts of his game will connect, Day has settled on a narrative theme. Players will control an intrepid prospector mining on Titan, Saturn's moon. They stumble on a vast network of caves—a classic dungeon-like setting Day is hoping to improve upon—and discover that the cave has a breathable atmosphere and livable temperatures. The next logical step is to go spelunking. Moments after they step the cave, the door slams shut, sealing them in the caverns.

Day believes the archetypical setting will give him plenty of room to subvert expectations.

> The advantage of the setting is that I have excuses for a number of standard tropes, and some unexpected things, too. I can have, for instance, cryogenically frozen lakes of liquid methane or whatever I need to have alongside floes of lava—both of which are potentially useful within the context of puzzles.

As players descend deeper into the cave system, Day hopes to reveal story bits every level or two. Stories, he points out, go over well in 7DRL challenges, since the very inclusion of a traditional narrative is enough to distinguish a roguelike from most of its peers. He wants to add a dash of mystery—a hook that, like the in-depth puzzle system he has planned, will pull players deeper into his world.

A few lynchpins are already in place. By his self-imposed deadline of 1:00 A.M., Day hopes to have dungeon generation more or less settled. The catch, he points out, is that most pieces of dungeon architecture must be moving parts—ones that players can manipulate in the service of the nascent, procedurally generated puzzle system.

> Getting these movable chunks of terrain, and getting them to tie into each other—so pushing one could, say, cause another to move in the opposite direction, or pushing one to the right causing another to move down; moves like those are the basic components the puzzles will rely on—is important.

He has named these movable pieces cogs, and the system of caves, Cronus. Appropriately, his game is now called *Cogs of Cronus*.

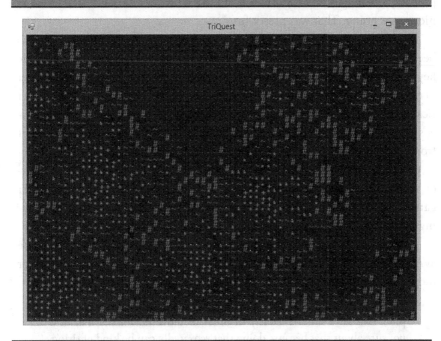

Cogs of Cronus. Every element, from the floor and walls to the enemies, will be a cog, all of which Joshua Day wants to be able to move around and play integral roles in puzzles (Image: Joshua Day).

Looking ahead to the events clogging his calendar—most notably an overnight trip to New York—Day knows what must be done first, second, and down the line. He stresses that the puzzle system *must* be in place by the end of day two for him to have any chance of the final product matching his bold vision.

Fortunately, he has a tentative plan. He wants to implement an abstract type of dungeon-generation system, where cogs are groups of cells independent of the map on the player's screen. That way, players and monsters alike will be able to interact with the cogs.

> One bit of leeway I have is that dungeon generation doesn't have to be working at this phase. As long as I can have a few chunks of things that move around in the way I've described, I can focus on creating other components that work with them in a temporary implementation. Then I can progress to get in the melee combat I described, and the monsters.

Yuji Kosugi and Carles Salas

Game: *Versus Time*
Date: Sunday, March 10th—Monday, March 11th

When I catch up with Kosugi, he sounds exhausted yet satisfied. "I've been programming for about 11 hours. People code for longer, but this is probably the longest, consecutive period I've written code. But I did get some nice tunes going. That was pretty fun."

Versus Time is in an embryonic state. Support for two human players has been implemented, and both are able to move around a dungeon using the keyboard. Enemies meander about as well; Kosugi plugged in routines to let players and enemies attack and, if their hit points reach zero, die. A timer ticks away during each player's turn, and letting it expire results in that player's demise, infusing each move with the urgency Kosugi wanted to import from blitz chess.

One issue weighing on Kosugi has been whether to implement four- or eight-directional movement. Since he is designing a local multiplayer game—wisely deciding that implementing online multiplayer would be biting off more than he could chew—all players must share a single keyboard. At present, player one moves using the arrow keys, and player two uses the WASD keys. Fewer keys per player would allow Kosugi to add support for more players, but could make movement cumbersome.

> The thing I've been trying is using four directions, and having people press two keys simultaneously in order to move diagonally. I'm now not sure about that because doing that repeatedly can be kind of tiring. That might be because I've been testing my game too much, he admits.

Kosugi is quick to point out that as robust as *Versus Time* seems at this early stage, everything still needs to undergo several rounds of tuning. That is where Salas—who was online earlier for a pow wow with his partner before heading out to take care of other business—will come in. Once Kosugi crashes for some much-needed sleep, Salas will take over tinkering with the prototype to feel out whether monsters or players die too quickly or too slowly, and whether players receive too much or too little time each turn.

"I want to see if there's a combination of those [factors] that makes the game feel compelling," Kosugi explains. "Then, based on that, I think we can make a good decision about trying to add skills and additional features, or if we should just refine what we have."

When I ask what is on deck for tomorrow, Kosugi waffles.

> I'm starting to feel like the idea of having [skills] might be a little too much to tackle this week, especially with my limited time. I might turn out to be wrong about that. At the same time, I think there's a pretty good game in there without skill, and with more directional movement.

Grimm Bros. (Ash Monif, Randis Albion, Mark Domowicz)

Game: *Dungeon X: Flesh Wounds*
Date: Sunday, March 10th—Monday, March 11th

True to their word, Monif, Albion, and Domowicz kicked off their 7DRL at midnight on Sunday, mere hours after wrapping up our meet-and-greet session. "We planned out all our tasks, what we felt was important. And then we just got started. Throughout the day, everything changes, of course," Monif tells me, sounding chipper. He has reason to be. During the midnight meeting, the guys charted their course through the first couple of days, then felt confident enough to hit the hay. "I took a big sleep to try and charge up for it. I'm hoping to do 80-plus hours this week if I can. Just nonstop," Domowicz says.

Domowicz woke up refreshed and promptly added the first monster Albion had drawn: a tree-stump able to camouflage itself in the forest, *Dungeon X*'s starting area, and attack unwary players. Domowicz is uncertain if the monster's camouflage ability will be present in their 7DRL build of the game, but the monster is ambulatory and able to attack the game's Red Riding Hood-like heroine.

With the first monster present and accounted for, the three developers dive into their respective jobs. "We're going to be working on the gameplay itself," Domowicz tells me when I asked about the rest of the day-one tasks on his agenda.

> We've been working on a results screen, which shows what happens after you die. Nothing happens when you die right now because it's just a tech demo. We need a high-score table as well. That's the major focus change from yesterday.

"I made a new monster, I checked in animation sets, and I painted a portrait for a new monster because we show you [monster portraits] when you attack them," Albion explains. "Then I wrote dialogue for the speech bubbles for all the existing monsters and characters. Now I'm making designs for the next monster. I'm going to continue working on game assets, props and stuff."

The Grimm team is filtering every line of code and designing every piece of artwork through the tone and theme they chose for *Dungeon X*. "We want our story to be dark and have black humor, but easily accessible. Think Monty Python and the Holy Grail, and Evil Dead. That's kind of the vibe we're going for," Monif describes.

Ido Yehieli

Game: *Fisticuffsmanship*
Date: Saturday, March 9th—Sunday, March 10th

Yehieli had earmarked the first weekend of the challenge as the ideal time during which to write the core mechanics of *Fisticuffsmanship*—awarding bonuses to the player's attacks and defense stats depending on his surroundings and movements. By the time we connect for our check-in, Yehieli has a game up and running, but feels his design still has a long way to go. "It turned out to be a little confusing to play," he admits.

I ask him to break down what has him discouraged. Yehieli explains that every time players move or attack, *Fisticuffsmanship* calculates how their previous movement benefits their attack or defense. For instance, players who stand their ground in a corridor while attacking earn extra defense, while moving in the same direction several turns in a row increases attack. (Yehieli has designs for more than nine such modifiers so that virtually any move the player makes will inform their attack or defense in some way.)

After calculating the player's action (or inaction), the game displays a message at the beginning of their *current* turn that informs them of the boon they received from their *previous* turn. Even Yehieli, the game's author, had trouble correlating the action from one turn ago to the turn unfolding in the present. The disconnect is understandable: players take a turn, and then watch the monsters move scurry about, studying their movements and devising a strategy to counteract them. But once their turn comes back around, they receive a message that yanks them out of the present, intruding on their thoughts and causing confusion.

Rather than alter how the game calculates stat gains, Yehieli wants to modify the messaging system to more clearly connect the player's action to his location.

I'll have to modify it to maybe only show the bonuses you get from your location in the map. That's something you can [more easily understand], and the bonuses you get from the move itself, I'll just describe in words. Like, 'You charge, so you get +2 to attack' or 'You attack from a sheltered position, so you get a boost to defense.' Stuff like that.

Despite his confusion, Yehieli seems content with the work he accomplished on day one.

Probably tomorrow evening when I get back to working on it, I'll work on the interface a little bit. Hopefully I'll be able to get most of the rest of the features implemented on Friday, which will be my next full day working on it. I plan to use that day for fixing and balancing.

Joseph Bradshaw

Game: *KlingonRL*
Date: Sunday, March 10th—Monday, March 11th

To stretch his mental muscles after years of severe allergies had left him bedridden, Bradshaw returned to writing games for the 7DRL challenge. To push himself physically, he took up an activity most adults put off for as long as possible.

"Just got done doing yard work. Daylight Savings Time kept me out there a lot longer," he greets me beamishly.

Staying up late the night before, he put together a prototype of *KlingonRL* that looks positively primordial: a screen filled with letters and symbols. In other words, how most roguelikes look when they hatch. As of today, a foundation is in place, giving him something he can build on as the 7DRL clock ticks away.

I got the sector map done. I also figured out what sizes everything needs to be. When you put everything on screen, it can be too small sometimes. Some roguelikes will do that. I've got the ship moving around on the map. So there you go, he finishes.

"I've got a randomized sector with different stars, and the ship moving around. Everything's looking good. It's perfect."

The sector map fills the screen. Twenty-six star systems—each represented by a large, colored asterisk—cover the map. Naturally, the player's ship is represented by an "@" symbol. When players bump a star system, the game will zoom in on a star system populated with procedurally generated enemies and objects—if all goes according to Bradshaw's design.

It's kind of a *GameMaker* thing: jumping between screens can be an issue. Scrolling is great, but jumping screens sometimes [causes problems]. Then I need to create the star system and save all 26 systems. I won't create them until you enter them, just to save on a big loading time at the beginning.

Brimming with energy, he plans to stay up for another 4 or 5 hours working. I leave him to it.

•

3

Day Two: Workday Blues

Darren Grey

Game: *Mosaic*

Date: Monday, March 11th—Tuesday, March 12th

Grey had counted on a long day at the office, and his prediction panned out. Fortunately, the workday was not a total loss.

> My plan—and I don't know if this will work because I've never done sound in a game, so this might be biting off more than I can chew—is that as you're wandering the map and laying down mosaic tiles, they're all leaving [musical] notes in a sequence that gets played in real-time. There's a sequencer playing your tiles as you move around. Hopefully that will sound nice instead of horrendous.

During downtime at work, Grey brainstormed ways to incorporate music in *Mosaic.* "I was listening to a lot of Pachelbel's Canon in D. I was thinking, *This is how I want my game to work.*"

Written by German composer Johann Pachelbel sometime in the late 1600s, Canon in D garnered far greater admiration following the composer's death in 1707 than while he was alive, as was the case for much of the classical music written during that era. A canon is a musical piece in which instruments play the same music but start at different times, blending together to create a sort of harmonious echo.

Pachelbel had dealt chiefly in organ and piano music, but accented his Canon in D with bass instruments. The piece was first published in 1919. It became an instant classic, and has maintained popularity providing the backbone of pop

DOI: 10.1201/9781003196723-3

songs produced by artists ranging from Tupac and Coolio to Green Day and Mary-Kate and Ashley Olsen. However, Pachelbel's Canon in D is most commonly heard during weddings as guests take their seats prior to the ceremony.

Grey daydreamed of creating the same effect for *Mosaic*.

> If I can get something sounding like Canon D, but generated automatically by a computer game based on how you're playing, that might be quite nice. That is immensely over-ambitious. It's going to be noise. It's going to be horrible. But that is the dream.

Lacking the energy for intensive coding back at home late that night, he sticks to toying with the rectangular outlines he drew the previous day. Each outline skews the base model's perfect rectangular form to varying degrees, resulting in greater visual diversity for the tiles on the map grid.

> I made about 24 or 25 [outlines], and then rotated them three different ways so I had about 100. Then I worked with the generator to produce these tiles in different colors. I went through a paint program and found some good palettes. The end result is I can now have about 100 million tile types in the game that can be generated. That's slightly too many, he finishes, sounding amused.

Then he shares his plan to revolutionize the standard form of the roguelike avatar. "I also played around with trying to combine an '@' symbol with a treble clef. This is the sort of thing that happens when it's 2:00 A.M. and your brain can't concentrate on coding anymore."

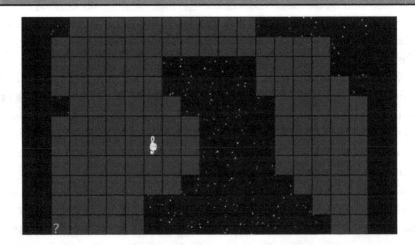

Mosaic. The player-character, an "@" symbol with a treble clef threaded through it, sits on an empty grid. Each time players move… (Image: Darren Grey)

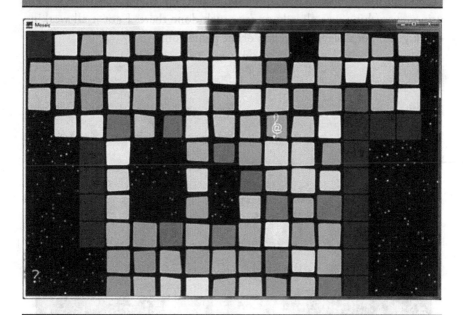

... the tiles will turn a different color (Image: Darren Grey).

Though daunted by the prospect of deploying audio during a week already jam-packed with responsibilities, Grey can think of no better time to experiment.

> One thing about a 7DRL is you tend to do something new. You try to improve your coding skills. When I made *Broken Bottle*, I'd never made a game with an experience system before, or an item system, or a game with consumables. I hadn't made a game with a proper story, either. I learned all these things while working on that game.

Bastien Gorissen

Game: *BattleRL*

Date: Monday, March 11th—Tuesday, March 12th

Like many other 7DRL developers, Gorissen has devoted most of his time to work but is still on target. Immediately after implementing his map, he implemented his "@" avatar and traversed the barren island, scouting ideal locations to plant buildings and weapon caches. But that, he says, is a job for later in the week. With a player-character to control, he concentrates on getting a better appreciation for how it feels to move around his budding world.

Writing field-of-view calculations ended up simpler than he anticipated. "I thought that would take me quite some time, but thanks to the library I'm using, everything was already pretty much done there. I got it all working quickly and got a playable version of the game going."

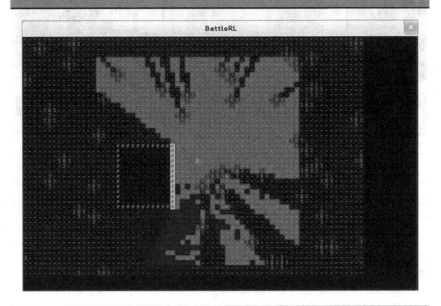

BattleRL, day two. The bright green "@" near the center of the map represents the player. Colored areas represent terrain the player can see from his position. Blackened areas, such as the space around and beside the building on the left, are out of his line of sight.

Although irritated that he cannot devote even more time to *BattleRL*, he confirms that he is pleased by what he has accomplished so far. What he hopes to do later in the week is captivate players despite the primitive graphical veneer inherent in the roguelike genre.

Of the roguelike genre's many game systems, procedural generation and permadeath are the most popular. Unsurprisingly, ASCII graphics turn up less frequently, particularly among publishers who know that a pretty face attracts mainstream attention more than a sparkling personality.

Dwarf Fortress stands as an exception to the rule. Released in 2006, the ASCII-based game asks players to generate an entire continent and manage a colony of dwarves from threats. Bastien Gorissen, another newcomer to the 7DRL scene, appreciated how the text graphics managed to engage him right off the bat.

> They were kind of clear, and you could use your imagination to enhance what you saw on the screen. The graphics for the dwarves were just little smiley faces, but you could picture them in any way you liked. Also, there was much information conveyed in simple terms. I quite liked that, he finishes, explaining that he hopes to draw players into the world he is creating in a similar fashion.

Before drawing our conversation to a close, I ask Gorissen what he believes might give him the most trouble as the challenge rolls on.

> I think it will be the last 10 percent of the game: polishing everything, and making sure everything works. I think level generation should go all right. I'm a little bit afraid of balancing everything, like difficulty. I think that will be the most difficult [aspect] for me.

Edward Kolis

Game: *TriQuest*
Date: Sunday, March 10th—Monday, March 11th

At the end of our previous check-in, Kolis predicted that implementing heroes would prove tougher than map generation, which he accomplished fairly quickly. To his surprise, that is not what is tripping him up.

> I spent a couple of hours on [the game]; it took a bit longer than I thought. In fact, I didn't quite get done everything that I wanted to. I should probably take a break; I'm getting a little tired from fiddling with this.

The snag has to do with displaying the map. In most roguelikes, maps are made up of simple grids consisting of tiles, and each tile can hold one object at a time (such as a character, monster, or item). *TriQuest* breaks its map into tiles *within tiles*, known as sub-tiles, to accommodate groups of characters, such as the player's party of three: when the player's trio of hero occupies a tile, each *individual* character stands on a sub-tile.

All those tiles and sub-tiles bogged down Kolis's map-display routine.

> When I tried to render the whole map at once at this higher resolution of nine sub-tiles per tile, it's 100 tiles across, so that's 300 by 300. That's a lot of rendering. I didn't have it set to clip stuff that's not on the screen.

He solved the problem by limiting the player's view. Rather than view the whole map at once, players see five squares—with a square being a group of sub-tiles within tiles—in every direction. As players move, squares no longer within view turn black. The solution forced Kolis to think about how to store terrain players have seen; if players leave a potion behind, the map must remember the coordinates of the potion so they can circle back for it later.

As a tentative solution, Kolis inserted a minimap into one-quarter of the screen. Presently, the minimap grants players the same five-squares-around vantage as the main map. Kolis plans to tweak it later on in the week so that it shows every square players have visited.

Despite the stumbling block, Kolis is confident he is still on track. Programming heroes was played a major part on his to-do list, and he was able to cross it off, but that doesn't mean he is completely satisfied with his progress.

> One other thing I didn't get to—I'll probably get to it later today or else later this week—is rearranging your formation. The nine tiles map to digit keys on the [keyboard's] number pad. You press a key to rearrange a formation, then type where your three characters go in whatever order you want them: warrior, mage, priest, or whatever. If you want the warrior up front, you assign him the first spot. I haven't done that part yet, but I'll get to it later.

TriQuest, day two. The map is cleaner and shows the player (represented by the red "@" symbol) in the center. Only the terrain adjacent to the player is shown. Players can consult the minimap in the upper-right corner for a broader view.

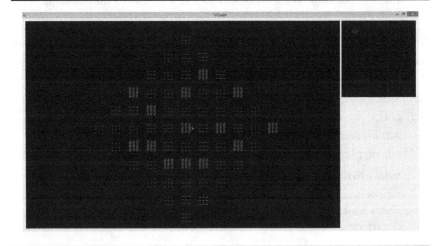

Joshua Day

Game: *Cogs of Cronus*
Date: Monday, March 11th—Tuesday, March 12th

I came to appreciate Day's views on what constitutes good news or bad news within the context of 7DRL challenges. On day zero, he told me—in good humor—that the offer he and his wife had made on a house had fallen through. Good news, he declared, since sealing the deal would have tied him up in more paperwork, which would have been one more obstacle between him and a finished 7DRL game.

On Monday, Day greets me with a bittersweet announcement sweeter than it is bitter. "I lost quite amount of time to a very good event, which is that a job I was waiting on looks like it's going to come through."

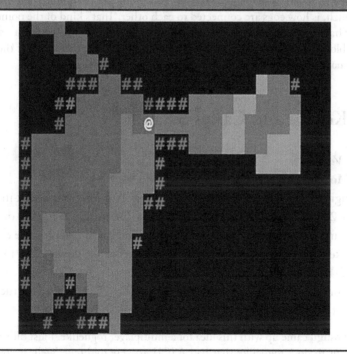

Cogs of Cronus. Different colors represent terrain such as lava and stone (Image: Joshua Day).

True to form, Day accepted the job with grace but kept mum on his chief concern: that his new employer would want him to start immediately, forcing him to set *Cogs of Cronus* aside. When the conversation ended, he breathed a sigh of relief. The job was a lock, but management still needed to iron out the details of his offer. Day had more time, and he would need every last second of it.

Implementing cogs had been Day's focus in the short span of time since we last touched base. Everything, he explains, is a cog: the player-character, the monsters, the moving walls, the pressure plates that cause walls and doors to move around—even the floor itself consists of multiple cogs so that every individual tile can be manipulated.

"Today was mostly spent getting the cog system working sensibly and hooking that up to some preliminary map generation," Day says before launching into a more detailed overview of how he envisions the cog system working. Every cog is made up of a rectangular body of cells, and each body of cells has a name and reference number. At a moment's notice, Day can refer to, say, a portion of the dungeon wall in the upper-left quadrant of the map, and command it to respond to the touch of another cog: the player, a monster, and so on.

Much of the system's underpinnings are in place, but Day has a great deal of work in front of him.

> One issue I'm still trying to sort out, and trying not to complicate it too much, is how cogs are connected to each other. That's kind of the point of having them. For instance, when you walk up to a pushing point on a block of cells and start pushing it, the game is supposed to treat the situation as if you've become linked with that block of cogs.

Yuji Kosugi and Carles Salas

Game: *Versus Time*
Date: Monday, March 11th—Tuesday, March 12th

Kosugi and Salas do not have much to report during our check-in. Over the past 2 days, Salas logged several hours in Photoshop, painting dungeon architecture and tiny characters for enemies and player avatars. He explains that he keeps a text editor open while he paints to jot down ideas for other artwork that come to mind.

Fashioning graphics for their roguelike, rather than relying on the time-honored tradition of text-based interfaces, is important to Salas.

> [Kosugi] came up with this idea for a multiplayer roguelike. I just didn't want to do a roguelike that had ASCII art. He told me, 'Well, if you think you can do the art...' and I just volunteered. I know it's blasphemy, but I can't stand ASCII graphics.

Kosugi and Salas share a desire to create something fresh.

Recently, I haven't been playing as many roguelikes. I've been really into competitive board games. I've been playing all kinds, inviting people over and playing stuff online. When this challenge came up, I tried to think of a way I could take the roguelike genre and make it into a competitive multiplayer game.

Salas chimes in:

> Since I'm not actually an artist—I just wanted art [in our 7DRL game] so I wouldn't have to look at [text] characters—I'm doing something very, very simple based on polygons. We have this knight, and he has a cube as a face, two little triangles for legs, things like that. I think it's better to think of something that's easy to recognize on a first glance, and think, *Okay, that's a warrior, that's a wolf.* They're colorful, easy-to-recognize polygons.

With the first weekend of the challenge in the bag, Kosugi's day job consumed the brunt of day two. He did have some good news, however. "I started implementing a skill system. Right now it's just a user interface [UI] for skills so you can cycle through and activate them, although they don't actually do anything."

Grimm Bros. (Ash Monif, Randis Albion, Mark Domowicz)

Game: *Dungeon X: Flesh Wounds*
Date: Monday, March 11th—Tuesday, March 12th

The words "How's everyone doing this evening?" have barely left my mouth before Domowicz cuts right to the chase. "I'm a little bit stressed right now because I'm working on something simple, but it's giving me problems." The fly in Domowicz's ointment is a user interface (UI) element, a counter that shows the player how much gold they have. For reasons proving to be unfathomable to Domowicz, the indicator refuses to show the correct number.

Other tasks are proceeding more smoothly. Domowicz has been busy writing level-generation algorithms for the caves players will explore in the 7DRL version of *Dungeon X*. Levels will be assembled in what he refers to as a level tree:

Dungeon X: Flesh Wounds. Robin, the player-character, confronts a skeleton in the forest, where players begin their adventure. Her pet, a wolf, waits for a chance to strike (Image: Grimm Bros., LLC).

Before, the level tree, as I called it, had two levels: a top level, and a bottom level. That was the whole game. Now we have a top level, and the top level has five staircases, so we have five different sub-levels.

Players will start at the base level and descend any of the five staircases, which lead to sub-levels, from there.

Domowicz's engine is flexible enough to accommodate a huge variety of layouts and visual textures. Albion has been painting rough, organic-looking ground and walls to immerse players in the claustrophobic experience of dungeon-crawling their way through uncharted caves.

Thanks to a companion character painted by Albion, the player's red-hooded avatar will not have to go spelunking alone.

> This wolf is the pet of our first hero character. Our character we chose for the hero is Red Robin, a twist on Little Red Riding Hood, so we gave her this wolf as a pet because it's a nice twist, Albion explains. By the time we spoke, Domowicz had already integrated the wolf into the code and gone on a few hunts down in the dark.

With more characters popping up and levels taking shape, the Grimm team discusses the scope they have in mind for the 7DRL challenge. Ultimately, they want to provide players with dozens of hours of dungeon-crawling entertainment. Cognizant of the fact that they have no chance of realizing such a lofty scope by the end of the week, they decide to dial back their ambition for the competition. *Dungeon X* will end after so many turns; players will strive to see how many points they can rack up by the end of the game.

> Our question for players is: how do I spend my turns? Do I spend my turns getting this cool item over here, which might, say, turn me invisible? Or do I go straight ahead and try to fight the boss?

Domowicz expounds. "That comes from the fact that we don't have the time to make a full inventory system [for the challenge]. That'll give us some gameplay goals, which will create a full experience for the 7DRL."

Ido Yehieli

Game: *Fisticuffsmanship*
Date: Sunday, March 10th—Monday, March 11th

Yehieli revised the messaging portion of his UI easily enough, leaving the rest of his evening wide open. He filled the time by adding weapons to *Fisticuffsmanship*.

While he stresses that equipment will play second fiddle to positioning and movement, tools of the trade such as knives and clubs still come in handy. Ordinarily in games, weapons are glorified containers for numbers: the knife inflicts more damage than the fist, while the short sword cuts deeper than the knife, and so on up the food chain. In *Fisticuffsmanship*, each weapon will feature usage patterns designed to influence how players move and position themselves.

"For example, the knife benefits from continuous use. It only has a couple turns in memory, but within those turns, the more you use it, the more damage it does," Yehieli explains. "Whereas the hammer benefits from long waits: if you haven't used it in a while, it does more damage, but if you continue using it, it does decreasing amounts of damage because you get tired from using it."

Yehieli promises that every weapon will exhibit a unique usage pattern, encouraging experimentation. Players will need to give serious thought before switching weapons, however, as picking up a new weapon causes them to drop whatever they are currently holding. Of course, they can always backtrack if they decide they prefer a weapon they jettisoned earlier—bearing in mind that the act of backtracking will cause changes to their attack and defense stats, just like any other form of movement.

> The whole battle system really depends on your action patterns. If you move, if you just attack, if you stand still—you very rarely want to bump into enemies head on in this game. It's more like boxing: you try to land a punch, then you try to avoid the other guy for a bit.

Looking ahead to the work week, Yehieli informs me that he will only be able to work on his game in fits and spurts until Friday, his next full day of coding, and his fifth day on the 7DRL clock. He feels he has no reason to worry. "Things are looking up. If it goes this way through the rest of the week, I think it will go very well."

Joseph Bradshaw

Game: *KlingonRL*
Date: Monday, March 11th—Tuesday, March 12th

Bradshaw put in 5 hours the day before, and 5 hours the day before that. His body is holding up fine. *GameMaker*, however, is in need of a breather. As he predicted, the program is having trouble juggling all of his data.

> Transferring information between screens in *GameMaker* can be kind of sketchy. As soon as your ship encounters a star system, you want it to jump to that screen, or room. That room is filled with planets. I was having trouble making that happen.

KlingonRL's sector map. The green "@" in the bottom-right corner represents the player's ship. The player can steer the ship into any of the colored asterisks, which represent individual star systems. When the player bumps a star system...

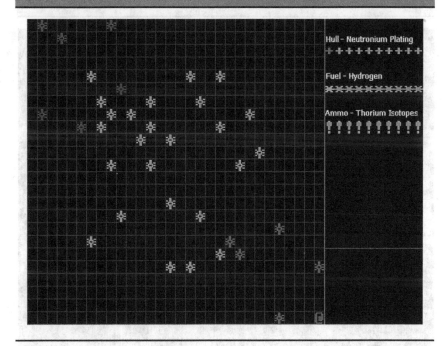

Bradshaw hooked on his programmer's tool belt and analyzed the problem. Players begin the game on the sector map, the main screen from which players can guide their ship toward individual star systems. Bradshaw had populated a master list—known as an "array" in programming jargon— with all the data pertaining to each star system, such as enemy ships and planets. His idea was to wait until players bumped into a star system to enter it, and then reference the array containing the data for that particular star system (enemy ships, planets, and other interactive objects), which would be displayed on the screen. For example, guiding the "@" ship to a star system in the bottom-right corner of the screen would fill the screen with a different layout of planets and enemies than, say, visiting a star system in the middle of the screen. Players would then leave the star system and return to the sector map, where they could explore another star system of their choosing.

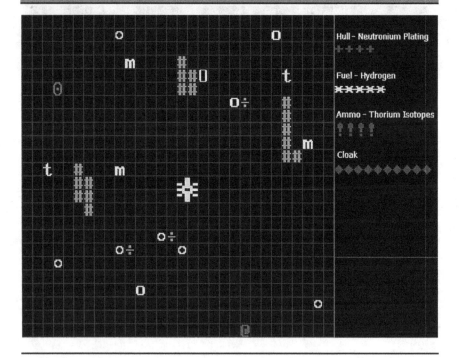

... they enter that star system, which contains an assortment of planets to mine for resources and enemies to fight.

Unfortunately, *GameMaker* had trouble pulling the data from the array of star systems. Earlier in the day, he attempted to soothe the problem away using logic. When that failed, he put his head down and barreled through it. Rather than dump data from arrays into a single room, he created 26 individual arrays and populated each one with data from a single star system.

"It's super inefficient, as it's saving an [entire] game state instead of just saving a few numbers in an array, but with roguelikes you can be inefficient due to the low system resources required [to play them]," Bradshaw reasons.

Though inelegant, his workaround does the trick, and that's all that matters when you have 1 week to build a complete game. Star systems now blossom on the screen each time he drifts into one of the asterisks on the sector map. Each one holds a combination of terrestrial planets, gas giants, and stars, and is fully navigable.

It took Bradshaw 1 hour to build the star-system generator. In the meantime, during our call, he fiddles with sizes for asteroid fields that occasionally pop up to give players trouble. For his next trick, he wants to add the bump interactions that occur when players knock against ships and other interactive objects. "That's super easy to do in GameMaker because there's a collision [routine] made for real-time, sprite-based games."

4

Day Three: Pressures

Darren Grey

Game: *Mosaic*

Date: Tuesday, March 12th—Wednesday, March 13th

Grey arrived at work at 7:00 in the morning and remained until 10:00 that evening. As soon as he got home, he diligently sat down at his computer. When our check-in chat begins, I am glad to hear that Grey used every waking hour to his advantage.

> It's always good to make use of idle time during the day to get a few ideas out. Sometimes when you're face to face with the code, it's hard to come up with ideas. If you have ideas earlier in the day, you should get them down so you make sure you don't forget them.

One of Grey's smarter ideas for *Mosaic* occurred early on in the planning stages. In addition to music, he wants to incorporate a series of *Street Fighter II*-like button sequences that raise lines of colored squares in specific directions, letting players stay a few steps ahead of aggressive enemies. "So, maybe pressing up-down-up-down will cause a string of tiles 10 tiles to appear vertically, rather than the four tiles you would have made otherwise," he suggests. He also has tentative plans to let players level up by giving them tiles that navigate the map independently, laying their own colored tiles as they go.

Grey's notes from earlier that day, typed in shorthand, have to do with enemy movement patterns and behavior, vital mechanics he has not yet programmed into *Mosaic*. He decides to ease players into the experience of

DOI: 10.1201/9781003196723-4

dealing with hostiles. "The first level won't have any enemies. It'll just have you playing about and making boxes. It's a playground level to get you used to moving your character and to understand the level-progression mechanism." Grey confided that he hopes players do not find traipsing around an empty grid "too boring," and that the experience of moving around and coloring in tiles will prove compelling on its own.

In level two, Grey plans for *Mosaic*'s first two monsters to make their entrance. Fittingly, their behavior will be straightforward. One of the capital letters will dance around erratically; the other will take the quickest route to the player. Grey promises that those foes will be easy to dispatch: simply walk around them to pen them in with colored squares. Tougher monsters introduced in subsequent levels will take more finesse to outmaneuver.

"What I don't want to do is just give it away," Gray explains.

> It's nice, when playing a game, to try to figure out systems for yourself. I don't want to just outright say, 'This is how you eliminate enemies.' I hope players will pick up on how enemies are behaving and how they can affect things.

Of course, all behaviors are mere daydreams at this point. Exhausted from the workday, Grey has yet to write any code for monster movement, and likely will not until tomorrow evening. He needs to spend time with his girlfriend, who he worries is feeling neglected between his long hours at work and the 7DRL commitment.

"It's not [coming together] as fast as I wanted, but I've got enough time in my schedule that that shouldn't be a big deal. I don't have a proper game yet, and I'll be much happier when I do."

Bastien Gorissen

Game: *BattleRL*
Date: Tuesday, March 12th—Wednesday, March 13th
"It's still going pretty well, but I'm starting to feel a bit more worried," Gorissen confesses. "Each time I do something, I think, *Oh, yeah, I need to do this too, and that needs to be in there, and...* The to-do list is growing more than it's shrinking."

Gorissen's stress springs from the combat system, which he has begun to implement. Thus far, he has given players the ability to engage enemies, and enemies possess the wherewithal to fight back.

It works great, at least for now. I haven't put much intelligence into enemies, so right now he's just moving randomly around the map, so you have to triangulate him and catch him. I also worked on the message system, so you have messages telling you if you hit the enemy or if he hit you.

BattleRL, day three. A rival student, Shinosuke Yamashita ("E"), goes toe to toe against the player's "@" avatar. The streaks of black represent terrain obscured by objects in front of them, limiting the player's field of view.

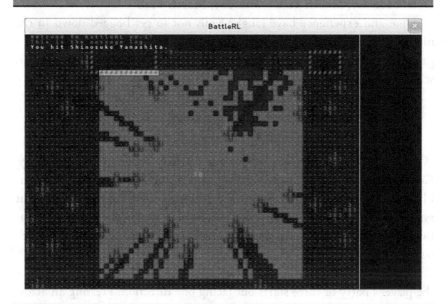

Between sparse hours to code in the mornings, long days at work, and fatigue from the day's activities, Gorissen struggles to keep his priorities straight. Every time his to-do list grows, intimidation sets in, and he finds himself fiddling with tasks he has already finished—a habit that will only delay implementing the components critical to finishing the core of *BattleRL*.

> I did have a couple of times—today and yesterday—where I had to say to myself, 'Okay, don't work on that anymore. It's working. Don't try to code it a better way or add too many bells and whistles.'

Combat needs to be expanded so computer-controlled characters can seek out adversaries and hunt for weapons such as clubs, knives, and guns. Time, the mechanism that controls when sections of the island will become forbidden zones, has yet to be applied.

He puts on a brave face at the end of our call.

> I still think I should be able to pull it off. I'm still confident, but I'm being careful not to include too many ideas. I need to keep things pretty basic so I can get the first version of everything working.

Edward Kolis

Game: *TriQuest*

Date: Monday, March 11th—Tuesday, March 12th

Time and experience have taught Kolis not to get bogged down in the nitty-gritty. The nitty-gritty must come later, after the main features of a game are playable. Fresh off the frustration of map-rendering, he sticks to his schedule and forges ahead.

> I added monsters to the game so you'll have something to fight. Well, [in previous incarnations] it was more like: if you bump into them, you kill them; if they bump into you, they kill you. So the game was very difficult!

What the primitive monsters lack in quality, they make up for in quantity. Kolis wrote code capable of generating several types of monsters and sprinkling them across the game map according to his danger-level gradient system. Still absent the intelligence to assemble into advantageous formations, monsters are at least able to lump together and attack the player's party.

Tactical movement will prove critical to survival in *TriQuest*. Each hero in the player's party of three starts out facing one direction. Pressing an arrow key *rotates* characters in that direction; pressing the same key again *moves* them in that direction. So if a monster attacks from the north, and players are facing west, they can press the up arrow key once to swivel north, placing the armored hero at the front of the party directly in line of their assailants, and protecting the weaker hero in the back. At the press of a key, heroes can rush up to the front to deal damage, or hunker down in the back.

Recognizing that there will be occasions where players want to move one way while facing another—for example, face west and sidle to the north—Kolis programmed a technique called strafe movement: hold Shift to prevent heroes from rotating while moving.

Kolis wants to give players the freedom to focus more on movement and formations and less on the minutia of combat, such as choosing which enemies to attack. Toward that end, he will keep things simple: bump into enemies, and the game does the rest. "Each [hero] will just pick its own target [in a formation], and if they all attack the same guy, so be it. It just depends on where the enemies are."

"I did design the final monster fight, which you encounter at level 10," Kolis tells me. The final monster lurks in a randomly chosen patch of the most dangerous terrain in *TriQuest*'s vast world. Players could stumble upon him at any time, but discretion is the better part of valor: players who take their time fighting monsters, which enables them to grow stronger and learn the skills they need to defeat foes in more dangerous areas, stand a higher chance of winning.

Joshua Day

Game: *Cogs of Cronus*
Date: Tuesday, March 12th—Wednesday, March 13th

Day is no stranger to ambitious game designs. *Rook*, a game he created for a previous 7DRL, riffed on the need to think several steps ahead in chess.[5] At the beginning of every turn, *Rook* evaluates every possible move players could make and forbids them from going in any direction that will kill them.

> It would copy the game board every time you made a move—all the monsters, the items, everything in your inventory, and you would all be copied. It would then step through the valid moves and then [factor in] each item in your inventory.

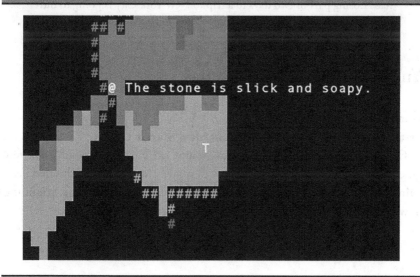

Cogs of Cronus. Here, the player manipulates stone cogs to solve a puzzle (Image: Joshua Day).

Cogs of Cronus is even larger in scope. This time around, however, Day may not be able to reconcile his big ideas with the realities of his schedule. Thursday afternoon and evening will be sacrificed to the New York trip, and the journey back home will consume Friday morning and afternoon. That leaves him two evenings plus the weekend to get the titular cogs of *Cogs of Cronus* linked together.

"One example of a piece I intend to use that way is a cube-shaped switch," he tells me, expounding on another type of cog he wanted to include in the game.

> It can only be represented as a single tile, but it has six faces to it. When you push it from a certain direction, rather than move, it will roll in place, performing the action that tilting a die from that angle would achieve. That would, of course, have six states.

From there, he could tie a cube-shaped switch into another cog that depended on which of the switch's six sides was facing up or down. For that to work, he explains, the framework of the cog system must be finished. It is not. "There's never any guarantee about that, especially in a seven-day challenge. I've had mixed results in the past with these big architectural gambles, but I still think they're worth making."

Sounding glum, Day runs through his schedule. Technically, he is only at the tail end of day two; he started at 10:00 P.M. on Sunday, and it is only 9:40 P.M. on Tuesday when we speak. He points out that his game already displays many of his design goals.

> You know, I'm talking myself into more confidence than I thought I had. Losing part of two days to a trip to New York City is going to hurt a little bit, but then I have the whole weekend to make up for it.

Yuji Kosugi and Carles Salas

Game: *Versus Time*
Date: Tuesday, March 12th—Wednesday, March 13th

On day three, pressures began to mount on Kosugi. Outside of a few quick chats with Salas concerning how to spawn the monsters Salas had been painting, "I'm going to have nothing for today," Kosugi tells me, sounding down. "It's been tough because I have work during the day."

Fortunately, he has given himself something to look forward to.

> I'm planning on taking a day off of work, either tomorrow or the day after, because I want an extra full day to code before Saturday. I'm hoping that [the day off from work] will be the day I'm able to implement the skill functionality—for players to use them, and for monsters as well.

Salas sounds just as discouraged. He painted a few tile sets *Versus Time* will use to construct dungeons, as well as a few monsters, but believes his inexperience creating art for video games is stunting his output.

> I actually wish I could have [finished] more monsters and more tile sets, but I'm struggling because the four or five monsters I have took me a lot of time. I know a proper artist could have done all of those in one day. It's a small amount of work for three or four days. It's kind of depressing when I see how small the amount of work is and how long everything took me.

Although Salas is vexed over his work rate, the work he *has* done will soon bear fruit. His first batch of monsters got lost in the background colors of the dungeon. Giving the matter some thought, he deduced that creatures needed more detail in order to stand out. Adding more color and surrounding the monsters in an outline enables players to spot them easily.

To Salas's delight, his work rate is improving. He spent the first day modeling a knight that looked "ugly," as he puts it. Deciding that his new monsters looked better, he made the call to set the knight and other day-one creations aside and concentrate on developing his speed and visual style for the rest of the monsters. "I did two monsters yesterday, so I am gaining speed."

Kosugi, meanwhile, has come to terms with the fact that there is only so much he can do on workdays.

> I'm mostly counting on the day off I take [later this week], and also Saturday, to get to the bulk of the remaining work. I don't deal well with sleep deprivation, so unlike a lot of people, I'm not going to try to stay up really late at night and work. I'd be miserable during the day and become less and less productive. But I do feel that, considering how much I got done on Saturday, I can replicate that over two full days later in the week. That'll leave me in pretty good shape.

Grimm Bros. (Ash Monif, Randis Albion, Mark Domowicz)

Game: *Dungeon X: Flesh Wounds*
Date: Tuesday, March 12th—Wednesday, March 13th

Hashing out game flow is still the prime objective when the Grimm team and I gather for our chat. Domowicz explains that they stuck with the decision to give players a finite amount of turns per game, and let the player decide how to spend them: explore, fight monsters, or get to the bottom of the trouble plaguing the irreverent fairytale-inspired world the team was creating.

> One of the big things I did last night was you can now win the game
> by defeating the boss, or you can lose by dying or running out of turns.
> Currently, when you die, the game takes you back to the beginning so
> you can have another go.

The boss in question is a giant slime, an enemy type that pays homage to a classic RPG enemy. In archetypal adventures such as *Dragon Warrior* on the Nintendo Entertainment System (NES), the blob-like slime is one of the earliest and weakest foes players encounter. For *Dungeon X*'s final boss, Albion conjured a giant blood slime, great and red and terrible. (The full release, due out at an undisclosed data after the 7DRL, will feature a different final boss.)

With a boss in place, Domowicz refined his dungeon algorithm. The cave-themed levels now consist of one large cave and four smaller ones, each a series of winding passages and cavernous halls.

"We're early in the 7DRL, so it feels pretty good. From this point on, it's going to be making things better: improving the combat system, adding items," Domowicz explains.

"We have a game loop. Now we can focus on making it a fun game loop." Monif echoes.

The blood slime joins a cadre of other monsters, so Albion declares the rogue's gallery finished.

Happy at the game's progress, Monif is leaving art and programming to Albion and Domowicz so he can tackle business-related tasks. "I'm doing a lot of business stuff; running the company, mostly," Monif explains. "I'm also play-testing. As soon as we get a new update, I grab the game and I play-test it. Every night, we go over feedback and make decisions together as a team regarding what's the most important priority."

Ido Yehieli

Game: *Fisticuffsmanship*
Date: Monday, March 11th—Tuesday, March 12th

A busy work schedule leaves Yehieli only 2 hours on Monday evening to work on his game. Rather than break new ground and let his foggy mind make a mess of the code, he decides he is far enough along to coast for a bit. He tracks down a few bugs, massages kinks in his algorithm for procedural dungeon generation, and continues streamlining the user interface (UI) in an effort to communicate what is transpiring on-screen as clearly as possible. With bug-hunting and UI-smoothing out of the way, "I improved the balance a little bit, and I implemented more weapons," he tells me.

We talk more about what drew Yehieli to roguelikes several years before. He explains that for all their underlying complexity, roguelikes appear simplistic on the surface. *Angband's* Spartan design appealed to Yehieli during his time studying mathematics in university.

> I played it, and quickly figured out it was something I could make by myself because it doesn't have any graphics or sounds; all I needed to do was know how to program. I came to appreciate a lot of the basic design principles behind roguelikes. I take them with me when I make other types of games.

When I ask him to expand on the design principles he carried with him from project to project, Yehieli gives the question some thought.

> One [principle] is randomizing the game every time you play it. You drastically increase the playability of the game, make it more interesting to play for longer, and produce interesting side effects. For example, you make the game much more complex through emergent complexity because you can expect [players] who are really into it to play it for years. People have been playing NetHack for over 20 years and they still don't win consistently.

Procedural generation—as applied to levels as well as rewards—feeds into what Yehieli sees as the bigger picture: game mechanics. Strip away expensive graphics engines and in-your-face stories, and the gameplay left over should be enough to keep players coming back. "Now, when I make any kind of game, the focus on game mechanics first and foremost is something that stays with me."

[*Author's Note*: Yehieli skipped day four of the challenge due to work..]

Joseph Bradshaw

Game: *KlingonRL*
Date: Tuesday, March 12th—Wednesday, March 13th

Bradshaw is up to his elbows in game mechanics. Fuel now drains from the player's ship when they move on the map-sector screen. Bumping into gas giants—found only within star systems—refuels their ship at the expense of hull plating, armor that absorbs two or three hits in combat. Planets can be raided to replenish ammo, and star bases patch up hull plating and top off fuel.

He finished all that work in just shy of 2 hours—proof that when *GameMaker* cooperates, it is precisely as efficient as Bradshaw expects.

> What I have next to do is bumping into and killing enemies, merchant ships, and bumping into neutral star bases and trading ammo for repairs. Those are all really easy; two or three lines of code each. That'll easily be done by tonight. Then it's just getting the ships to come after you, which is going to take all day. I might try to push through tonight. We'll see.

Bradshaw goes into more detail on how he envisions the artificial intelligence (A.I.) for enemy ships working out. Each enemy will cycle through one of three states: patrolling, attacking, or fleeing. Patrolling will cause enemies to move around somewhat drunkenly in one direction until they decide to reverse course.

He also wants to improve on what he views as the nebulous nature of roguelikes. Learning how to move around the screen in games such as *Rogue* and *NetHack* is just the first step, he reasons. Deciphering the function of every key on the keyboard, as well as ascertaining the precise cause of death when players fall victim to a new monster, are deterrents for new players.

> Every time you die [in *KlingonRL*], I want to give a message about why you died, and how not to die that way again. So if you run out of fuel, it'll say, 'You ran out of fuel and lost. Your ship runs on hydrogen. You can get hydrogen at gas giants or friendly star bases.' I'm not going to tell people you can refuel at stars; I'll let that be a little Easter egg.

I could not detect the slightest trace of anxiety in Bradshaw's tone. Finishing the game replete with every feature on his wish list seems a foregone conclusion.

I picked a good size, a good scope. Right now, since I know I'm going to be done tomorrow night—barring any major fiascos—so I'm adding features. I'm adding three sizes of planets right now. I'm doing graphical tweaks already. I foresee success and trying to get someone to test it pretty soon.

If worse comes to worst, Bradshaw has a Plan B. "Eight o'clock on Saturday night is when I started, but I'll be working until 9:00 this Saturday night because of Daylight Savings. That's some quick thinking there, huh?" he says with a laugh.

5

Day Four: Halfway

Darren Grey

Game: *Mosaic*
Date: Wednesday, March 13th—Thursday, March 14th

Unable to sleep much the night before, Grey called off from work, slept most of the day, and woke up refreshed and committed to making headway on *Mosaic*.

"You called me just as I broke the game. Again."

Grey knows he cannot heap too much blame on *Mosaic*. Before heading to bed the night before, he unwisely tried to implement a mechanic where, when players walk in a square-shaped pattern, the game fills in all the squares in the pattern with color. For reasons he had been unable to decipher until just before our Skype chat, the mechanic was not working.

> One of the problems with procedural content is it's not obvious what the hell is going on. You kind of have to keep trying different things and try to spot patterns in the algorithm, find a clear point at which it's failing. I eventually figured out what was wrong and fixed it.

But Grey's string of bad luck was not over yet. Moving on, he attempted to write the routines in charge of behavior for each enemy type. Rather than introducing new code in manageable chunks, he flooded his files with lines of code, many of which turned out to be faulty.

> Because I'm using Lua [the language in which the T-engine is written], you don't hit a compile button and get a list of errors. You run the

DOI: 10.1201/9781003196723-5

program, and you get an error, so you go and fix that error. You run the
program again, and you get another error. Lua can save you a lot of time
coding, but debugging takes a bit longer.

Grey sounds more tired than frustrated, though. As if he anticipated something like this might happen.

> I do a lot of trial-and-error coding, which is not the best way to code,
> but it works well enough for me. In these sorts of seven-day jams, you
> sort of have to be a bit dirty in how you code.

To his credit, the payoff sounds incredible. Grey has dreamed up devious
enemies to follow up on the simplistic ones that appear in the first few levels
of *Mosaic*. One enemy moves in circles, making it tricky to box in since players must take a long and circuitous route around it, potentially running into
other monsters along the way. Another enemy retreats from players each time
they take a step toward it.

> One of the most annoying [enemies] will be one that sticks to the edges
> at all times. It only moves around the edges. That will probably be one
> of the harder enemies to kill because you have to surround it.

One of Grey's favorite ideas, yet to be programmed, is a monster that shoves
players. As they fall back, they might collide with colored tiles they had created, leaving a gaping hole in their pattern—to their detriment if they were
trying to box in a monster.

> I'm going to maybe experiment with enemies that have different pat-
> terns of destruction. You'll have to plan quite a few moves ahead to
> make the most of your moves. But that should be intuitive at the same
> time because you're thinking in lines rather than single steps. It's not
> like chess, where you're thinking of each move. You can predict overall
> movement, thinking through turns very quickly.

That all sounds great—provided Grey can weed out his code in the 72 odd
hours left in the challenge.

Bastien Gorissen

Game: *BattleRL*
Date: Wednesday, March 13th—Thursday, March 14th
I catch up with Gorissen roughly one-quarter into his to-do list for the
day. He sat down to code with four tasks to complete but has only finished one: laying the groundwork for time and the myriad of ways it will

influence gameplay. Next, he wants to insert the mechanisms that close off portions of the island according to how much time remains.

"That's the thing I need to do right now: [decide] which zone I want to make forbidden to the player and other characters, and work to make them inaccessible after a set time." I detected an undercurrent of guilt as he went on, "Then I still need to do what I didn't do yesterday, which is ranged attacks. I was too tired, so I went to sleep."

Gorissen also wants to smarten up the artificial intelligence-controlled opponents that will be roaming the island. They are up and moving, but do so arbitrarily, leaving the player feeling unthreatened and able to explore at a leisurely pace. Tightening up the A.I. should not take long, provided he can stick to a lesson he heard on an episode of Roguelike Radio.

> Someone said you should keep things simple. Most of the time, when you see a character on the screen, it moves more or less randomly except if you do a lot of work on the A.I. Even if decision-making is really complex, characters still move somewhat randomly.

BattleRL, day four. Gorissen implemented time, shown as a counter on the right-hand side of the screen.

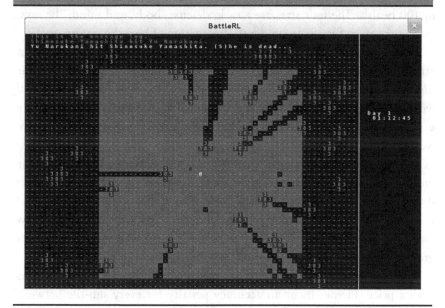

He knows how to proceed. At the beginning of every turn, each A.I. opponent will calculate its field of view. Then the game will draw lines from the opponents to every other part of the map. If one of those lines connects with an adversary, player-controlled or otherwise, it will set off in that direction. Should all the lines hit obstacles, the A.I.-controlled opponent will move randomly until its next turn, when it crunches the numbers again.

Provided he has time, Gorissen would love to capitalize on the human interactions in *Battle Royale* and *The Hunger Games*—an aspect of his game he hopes will shine through the rudimentary graphics.

> The people forced to fight to the death are students in the same class. It would be interesting if I could implement friendships in the beginning so that if two characters find each other, they help each other at first. That will be something to save for later if I have the time.

[Author's Note: Gorissen was too busy to talk on Day Five.]

Edward Kolis

Game: *TriQuest*
Date: Tuesday, March 12th—Wednesday, March 13th

One full day removed from our last chat finds Kolis delighted with his combat system. "Each creature, hero or monster, gets four stats in addition to 100 health. The four stats are attack, defense, body, and mind," he says, setting the stage for a more in-depth explanation of how the system works.

When a monster elects to attack, it determines whether to launch an attack based on the values of its mind and body stats. If the body stat is higher, the attack will be physical and vice versa. "I'm hoping that will work out. In my play-testing so far, it seems like weak monsters are really easy because they can barely defend and barely hit you—but, hey, they're weak monsters."

The player's tactical choices can heighten the difficulty as much as the greater threat posed by monsters in more dangerous areas. Success comes down to formation—the player's, as well as the stance adopted by a pack of monsters. For instance, it may behoove players to let a weaker monster gnaw away at their flank in order to let their heavily armored warrior stand his ground against the more threatening monster at the head of the pack.

Hiding in the back may offer more protection, but that protection comes with a price. Heroes incur an accuracy penalty for every sub-tile between them and their target. To keep things fair, Kolis applies that same penalty to monsters.

With a more concrete combat system in place, Kolis moves on to expanding the game loop: exploring the map, killing monsters, looting their corpses for equipment, and growing ever more capable of surviving in rougher areas such as deserts and wastelands. Better equipment increases the player's odds of survival, and tougher regions hold better equipment. Players will be able to carefully monitor their party's status via the stats box on the right-hand side of the screen, which lists each party member's vitals.

Naturally, the advent of a new system in the game introduces a fresh crop of problems to weed out. His current bugbear is a glitch that causes monsters to always attack the hero in the rear of the player's party, though the glitch is a minor issue.

> I feel pretty good. I've got a working game. All the stuff coming up next is to make the game cool: items, skills, and stuff. Even if I don't get that done, I've got a working game and can call the project a success. I just want to add things on to make it more interesting.

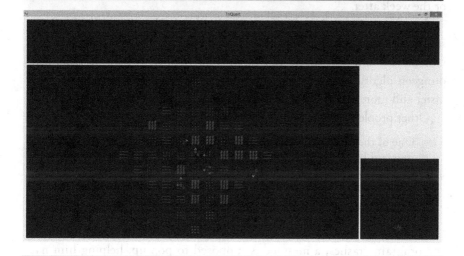

TriQuest, day four. The player's party skirts around mobs of monsters. The minimap has been moved to the lower-right corner.

Joshua Day

Game: *Cogs of Cronus*
Date: Wednesday, March 13th—Thursday, March 14th

Murphy's Law is in full effect at the Day household. He has yet to finish the cog-based puzzle system, and the components he *had* finished are misbehaving. Bugs are piling up. Then there's the upcoming trip to New York.

Packing, traveling, socializing—all activities that would keep him away from his computer.

Stress set in, gnawing at his concentration. He was so worried that *Cogs of Cronus* would not be finished in time that his anxiety was giving way to a self-fulfilling prophecy: each second he sat fretting caused the game to slip further and further behind schedule.

Thankfully, his wife saved the day. Curious about the process of writing a game, she sat down asked if she could watch him code. Having an attentive audience gave him the motivation he needed.

> I would ask her, 'What do you want me to add next? Of the things I've talked about, what should go into the game?' We went through the addition of items, an inventory, and things like that—things that really do only take 20 minutes or half an hour to do really well, but the focus you need during that time is just incredible. That's the whole point of the challenge: to focus.

When Day reached a stopping point, his wife broached the subject of post-poning the trip. They had yet to book their tickets. They could go next week, or the week after.

Day felt a great weight lift from his shoulders. He redoubled his efforts, stepping away from the increasingly intimidating cog system for the moment. Combat is working; players can bump into enemies to engage them. His dungeon algorithm has improved significantly; levels are coming together faster and more organically than before.

Other problems crop up, however.

> One of the problems I've been having is that I'm targeting curses, the standard library on Linux, and that mangles my error messages when I have a crash. They get dumped to the terminal, and the terminal is in curses mode, so everything gets written out funny. It takes a long time for me to read it.

Like many programmers, he coded error-handling into the game: when the program crashes, a message is supposed to pop up, helping him nar-row down the origin of the crash. But *Cogs of Cronus* refuses to throw him error messages, leaving him in the dark every time the game grinds to a halt. Drawing from a pool of renewed focus and energy, Day retools the message system. He solves the issue by copying some of the code he wrote to display the player's inventory and pasting it over his error-handling system.

Anytime an error happens during gameplay, it'll catch the error and bring up a big dialogue box and try to continue the game. So as long as it's an action you take while playing the game—maybe you attack and the game tries to divide by zero—the game can continue.

Doubling back, he returns to his dungeon-generation algorithms. They are stable but missing decor that he believes will heighten the theme of the game. His solution is to implement a masking system, a type of cover he can apply to walls and floors in order to mark them as open to receiving special details. "Once the whole dungeon was carved out, it could be populated with all the pretty decorations. Then I could have a separate mask generator that could generate rooms of different shapes."

Day believes carving rooms of varying shapes adds to the mystique of the cave system and lends a more organic look to each cave.

Initially I was using ellipsoid rooms, but I've moved on to a more natural splashing effect. I can have ellipsoid rooms, I can have rectangles, I can have natural cavern-shaped rooms, and they get placed on the map wherever they can without overlapping. Sometimes they naturally touch each other, and that creates connectivity.

After we hung up, I reflected on our conversation. Dungeons are built from cogs and seem to be taking shape. But the cog-based puzzles, the reason for *Cogs of Cronus*'s existence, still seemed too far away.

Yuji Kosugi and Carles Salas

Game: *Versus Time*
Date: Wednesday, March 13th—Thursday, March 14th

The day Kosugi has been waiting for has arrived. "I took the day off of work today, and I'm at [Salas's] place." Giddiness creeps into his voice. "So much programming. My brain is kind of melting." Immediately after arriving at Sala's apartment, Kosugi went on a coding bender for 10 straight hours, leading right into our Skype call.

"We took a short break for lunch," Salas adds. He pauses. "It was very short."

Kosugi's first order of business was to build on the skill system which he had started 2 days prior. In *Versus Time*, skills are special abilities such as fireballs and the ability to rest. The monsters surrounding them hold two skills each. When a monster dies, it drops its skills, and players can pick them up by touching them.

Kosugi's implementation of skills makes fighting monsters a powerful motivator: fighting monsters and laying claim to their dropped skills is critical to gaining an advantage against other players. That advantage is balanced by charging a heavy cost. Rather than mana energy, the standard magical resource in most RPGs, skills cost *time*, draining precious seconds off the player's timer. For instance, all players start with the Rest skill. Invoking it allows players to convert seconds into hit points—great for coming back from near-death encounters, but a heavy gamble for players who have their eye on a monster all the way on the other side of the screen and very little time to cross the distance.

Kosugi realizes that performing skills needs to be quick and effortless so that players can use their allotted time efficiently each turn. Therefore, skills either activate immediately upon pressing a key, or allow players to first select the direction a skill—such as a fireball—will be cast in.

He has ideas for skills beyond time-honored projectiles like fireballs. When I called, he was in the middle of coding the Create Wall skill, which raises a wall on the tile in front of the caster, shielding him or her from harm. Kosugi also has his eye on an invisibility skill. Any extra abilities will have to wait until the main game is done.

"In terms of making this into an actual game that's balanced and playable, the big thing I have to do is improve the monster spawning so that you don't start the game surrounded by monsters that will immediately kill you," he says.

Kosugi feels his relative inexperience writing code, and the 7DRL's tight deadline has prevented him from designing a more dynamic skill system. At the same time, he takes pride in extending the skill system to monsters. He wanted them to be "first-class citizens able to do the same things as players."

Salas speaks up. "There are a couple of monsters that, instead of giving you a skill, they give you an instant upgrade—either for your attack, or your maximum HP [hit points]."

The next step, they explain, is to collate all the pieces and fit them into a proper game. Kosugi has a tentative idea of how the game will start. Players will be able to move around and attack, and use a skill that lets them rest, restoring a small amount of hit points. Using the skill is risky, though, as it converts time into HP, and players die if their timer expires. If time allows, Kosugi hopes to circle back to his dungeon-generation algorithm, which he feels is turning out subpar levels.

Salas's mood is even more improved than his partner's. "I completed more stuff today than in the rest of the days together so far. I made five new monsters, and I've [drawn] all the skills. We have seven skill right now. I'm having a lot of fun."

Grimm Bros. (Ash Monif, Randis Albion, Mark Domowicz)

Game: *Dungeon X: Flesh Wounds*
Date: Wednesday, March 13th—Thursday, March 14th

Over the past 24 hours, Albion and Domowicz cranked out droves of power-ups to aid players in their quest through *Dungeon X*'s system of caves. Housekeeping tasks claim day four. "I spent a lot of time making the game portable: getting it to where we could take it out of the development environment and give it to anybody and have them play it," Domowicz recounts. "Things like that are kind of mundane, but they have to be done or we can't have a game."

It took Domowicz many hours of playing *NetHack* to understand just how intricately a roguelike's elements must be woven together.

> The game I was working on [prior to joining Grimm Bros.] was really complicated, so I got to looking at *NetHack* and thought, *Man, I should be doing this instead.* Clearly that was a mistake of reasoning; a good roguelike is a very in-depth project as well. But that was part of the allure, and I was having a lot of fun playing *NetHack*.

Even as the Grimm Bros. team gently separates *Dungeon X* from its apron strings, they have their eyes fixed on the road ahead. Sound effects have yet to be recorded and implemented; that is on the docket for tomorrow, by which time Monif hopes to have welcomed a composer into the fold. His choice: Jade Leamcharaskul, a musician and aspiring game designer who founded indie studio JDWasabi Studios, where she and a group of developers are working on horror-themed games.

Leamcharaskul was excited to sign a contract with Grimm Bros. but made it clear that her plate was filled with prior commitments that had to be cleared away first. Monif shares his hope that she will be able to record a few tracks and sound effects by the end of the week.

In the meantime, Monif is keeping busy motivating his team and handling assorted odds and ends on the business side. He wants *Dungeon X* to make a big splash when it's ready for its public appearance in the 7DRL spotlight.

> Everyone else is nose-to-the-grindstone on it; they're in the trenches. I'm looking at this as a whole project, asking myself, 'What does this game need?' I'm cheerleading, I'm supporting, and I'm testing. All these things combined together make up a good producer, and that's what I'm trying to be: humble, supportive, and cheering on my team members to do the best job they can.

Joseph Bradshaw

Game: *KlingonRL*
Date: Wednesday, March 13th—Thursday, March 14th

KlingonRL is finished. That, Bradshaw says, is the good news. The bad news: he does not find it fun.

Prior to our conversation, Bradshaw planted the Genesis Device in the game. Players could start a new session, fight their way to the device, retrieve it, and carry it back. The problem is the moment-to-moment gameplay. "There's not enough variety yet. Roguelikes get their fun factor from the interplay between procedural generation and permadeath, so every time you start, you want the game to be different. Not just a different layout."

Bradshaw plans to remedy that by sprinkling in rare events, a staple of roguelike games. Some rare events, such as discovering a powerful artifact item in an *Angband* dungeon, are boons for players. Others, such as *Rogue*'s cursed items, throw monkey wrenches into their progress. Bradshaw proposes to spice things up by throwing monkey wrenches such as pirate vessels and Federation cruisers that stand a chance of materializing in the player's current star system.

"I can have star bases fire missiles. All of this is very easy to do—10 or 15 minutes per thing. The real challenge now is making it hard enough and interesting enough."

Our conversation segued to his predilection for crafting intriguing and challenging games, a process that began long before he discovered the 7DRL. As a child, he invented a steady supply of board and card games that he played with friends. He admitted to me that none of them were good, but designing "good" games was not his objective. He was driven to create, and the 7DRL was a creative outlet.

For the 2010 7DRL, his first, Bradshaw created *Gunfist*. The game crossed sci-fi elements—his genre of choice—with the gameplay from *Gauntlet*, one of his favorite old-school arcade action games. Players guided a soldier armed with a laser around procedurally generated corridors, blasting enemies and saving civilians. The hook was that players got to watch little robots scuttle around the screen snapping architecture into place before each level started, giving them a chance to memorize the level before it began.

Bradshaw is just as excited about his current project as the ones from previous years. *KlingonRL* is done. But he will feel unfulfilled if he turns the game in now. He has devoted the entire day to tampering and wants to get a few more hours in before bed.

6

Day Five: Bugs

Darren Grey

Game: *Mosaic*
Date: Thursday, March 14th—Friday, March 15th

In the process of weeding out bugs and implementing mechanics, Grey's game has taken an unexpected turn.

> When I put my initial design together, how I envisioned it, I found it was kind of along the lines of impossibly hard. The way I could get it to be easier to test was to halve the speed of all the enemies and reduce the enemy spawn rate by 90 percent. So it's an easy build right now. I'll have to round up the difficulty a bit more.

The trouble is that monsters are too easy to defeat. Level after level, he emerged victorious by hugging the closest wall and running along the edges of the map, filling in the entire map and vanquishing enemies in one fell swoop. Grey assures me that conquering the final incarnation of *Mosaic* will not be so simple. "I assume everyone moves in straight lines, so you'll figure that one out quickly."

What he really wants to know is if he should clue players in to other movement patterns. That line between accessibility and figure-it-out-yourself challenge has always been a fine one to walk for Grey, as well as hundreds of other experienced game designers.

DOI: 10.1201/9781003196723-6

Mosaic. **Box-in enemies with colored tiles to defeat them (Image: Darren Grey).**

To solve the problem, he will fall back on his penchant for keeping controls simple and dialing up the difficulty—manifested via cunning enemy movement patterns. In most of Grey's 7DRL games, all of the commands at the player's disposal are mapped to the number pad. *Mosaic* will follow suit.

> I think a lot of roguelikes, especially of the *NetHack* variety, have this complexity through the different commands you can do. But during the game, you very rarely use the full range of commands, so interface-wise it doesn't work out very well. Sometimes it feels like false complexity: you're given all these commands, but 99 percent of the time, all you're going to do is bump into things.

Thus far, Grey has straightened out code for two of the enemies in the game. He wants to add eight more. While ten monsters are fewer than many roguelikes contain, Grey believes the combination of facing several enemies in the same level, each with its own behavior, will keep players' hands full.

To complement the player's ability to pen in enemies by tracing squares around them, Grey has programmed in a few sequences, with more to come over the next couple of days. "For example, pressing up-left-down-right, moving in a little circle, will create a large circle of tiles all around you.

It's one move I have planned to put in. They're quite quick to code. The basics are in there."

The rest of the items on Grey's to-do list will require lots of heavy lifting. He wants to add progression from level to level so that players get a sense of continuity as they progress. He would also like to create some kind of scoring mechanic—not an explicit high-score counter, but a way for players to track how far they get in the game. Currently, *Mosaic* tells players how many levels they finished; Grey wants to track information more closely.

He is also frustrated by an odd glitch. The game's background, on which tiles are displayed, consists of a field of stars that scrolls by slowly. For some reason, the star field disappears in level two and on, leaving players with a plain black background. Another bug causes a single mosaic tile to appear next to players when they begin a new level. "I've got absolutely no idea why the hell the code does that," Grey admits, explaining that the bug persists even though he wrote code necessary to remove it.

Grey has deemed *Mosaic* far enough along to send it out to a few trusted friends who own computers across a spectrum of hardware. To his delight, the game moves smoothly even on older machines.

His last words before we signed off for the night proved prescient. "There's no sound in the game yet. That will be a last-day hack."

Edward Kolis

Game: *TriQuest*

Date: Wednesday, March 13th—Thursday, March 14th

TriQuest is rolling along smoothly. Per the tasks listed on his calendar, Kolis spent the day devising a skill system used by players and monsters. Each player receives two skills tailored to their role. Warriors hack away with omnislash, a sweeping attack that damages all enemies, and go into berserk mode, which increases his attack and body stats but lowers mind and defense. The mage throws fireballs and cuts enemy attack speed in half for a brief number of turns, while the priest banishes enemies to a random corner of the map and restores hit points to his comrades.

While skills are working as advertised, Kolis feels he needs to massage the numbers a bit, as some skills feel overpowered. The warrior's Omnislash is a powerful strike that never misses regardless of the range between the warrior and his prey. Similarly, the mage casts fireballs that always hit their mark no matter how far away. To compensate for the efficacy of these and other skills, Kolis will only allow players to a single skill per turn. Players will have to think carefully over which hero's skill will best serve their situation: should the priest heal the party's wounds, or should the warrior wreak havoc with Omnislash?

I asked Kolis what he had in mind for tomorrow. He responded without hesitation: item implementation, a task that will either go smoothly or erect a high hurdle. What he wants is for monsters to drop items consistent with their danger level. Weak monsters will drop basic equipment, and stronger monsters will leave behind better loot.

Interestingly, Kolis wants to differentiate items from weapons and armor on a molecular level. He cites Nintendo's *Super Mario Bros.* series of platform games as his working example. In a *Mario* game, players consume a power-up the moment they touch it, rather than being given the option to save it for later. Items will work the same way in *TriQuest*, Kolis explains. He believes programming an inventory will take too much time and wants to keep players focused on making tactical decisions instead of rooting through menus.

Kolis is carrying that mindset over to armor and weapons. In most roguelikes, players can pick up multiples of each item—such as swords and chainmail vests—and sell the excess for gold in town. *TriQuest* will not contain vendors or an economy, so Kolis sees no reason to let players pick up more than one of each armor and weapon type.

"What's the point of having two chainmail suits?" he reasons. "It's not like one of them is going to break; I won't have that kind of mechanic." Instead, the differences will be fundamental. Heavy armor might slow players down, and the mage might be able to find staffs that inflict different types of elemental damage.

"That'll make it more interesting than just, 'this one is better than that one,'" Kolis says, anticipating the challenge day six will bring.

Joshua Day

Game: *Cogs of Cronus*
Date: Thursday, March 14th—Friday, March 15th

"The trip to New York ended up happening," Day admits. And that, he goes on, was a good thing.

Far from stealing precious hours, the trip bequeathed time. Traveling by train, Day was afforded blessing: the wireless Internet in his car was on the blink. Eight distraction-free hours—four there, four back—stretched in front of him. He took full advantage, checking off several boxes during the trip.

First up on the itinerary was a new bug that had surfaced in his dungeon algorithm, one subtle enough to allow the game to continue chugging along rather than bring it crashing down. In a way, Day knew, subtle bugs were the worst breed. If a game crashed, at least it was obvious that something had gone wrong. Logic bugs burrowed deeper in the code, infesting components in ways that often went undetected until long after the game had been released for public consumption.

Fortunately, Day had been granted a surfeit of time. "The algorithm I came up with was one where it starts, checks that everything is connected, and if it's not, it takes an action that's supposed to get things closer to all being connected. Then it checks again," he explained, adding that this whole process rinses and repeats until the whole dungeon is assembled.

Except the algorithm was *not* rinsing and repeating, nor going through a full cycle even once. The stage at which walls, floors, and various other cogs were supposed to be linked was all smoke and mirrors. Dungeon levels materialized on the screen and could be explored, but the links joining cogs went unconnected. Day tracked down the issue and corrected it: cogs could now be linked, although the cog system had yet to be finished.

Back home from the trip, Day adds a new wrinkle to navigation. "I implemented auto-run today, which is a handy feature for any keyboard player. There are details with that to sort out; detecting which position [the avatar] needs to stop running in, and so forth." Using auto-run, players can traverse open ground with a single key press rather than having to tap the same arrow over and over to cover huge swatches of open space.

Surprisingly, implementing the critical cog-based puzzles is not next on his schedule. Instead, he is working on doors and levers. Those, Day explains, are two of many items remaining on his list of odds and ends. He also needs to tighten up the messaging system that will communicate actions to players— the outcome of triggering a trap or pulling a switch, damage dealt to and received from monsters, picking up items, and so forth. That is on the table for tomorrow.

Completing little goals will help the game feel more polished and complete, Day believes.

The other thing I'm looking at, in addition to spreading around things like foliage and other features, like water—which will make dungeons feel so much more alive—is I want to get sort of a marble texture applied to the walls so that every level will have a couple colors of wall and floor, and feel sedimentary.

Yuji Kosugi and Carles Salas

Game: *Versus Time*
Date: Thursday, March 14th—Friday, March 15th
Kosugi is speeding up instead of slowing down.

> I've been surprisingly productive since getting home from work. While I was at work, [Salas] was testing the game a bit. We noticed a couple of big bugs. Every time we made a move, the speed at which your time depleted got faster and faster. You'd lose seconds at a rate faster than actual time.

With the game's timer now depleting at an acceptable speed, Kosugi and Salas ride their wave of momentum to the next bug, which gives monsters a surplus of life when they appear.

Once monsters were once again manageable, the developers split up to tackle separate tasks. Salas initially concentrates on painting the user interface (UI). The UI is one of the most important elements in a game, as it communicates critical information such as how much life and time players have remaining. Even veteran designers run themselves ragged trying to construct an interface that conveys information without getting in the way of the on-screen action, and in a way that is easily understood. *Versus Time* demands twice the elegance of a two-player game: since up to four players can join in, a single UI has to communicate information for all four players at once.

Salas struggles for a couple of hours before setting the UI aside and focusing on play-testing the latest version of *Versus Time*.

> I've been toying with the balancing this afternoon, trying to make [the game] more survivable. I want to see if tweaking skill costs and monster damage, things like that, will make it less difficult than it is right now. Now, people could only kill one monster; unless they heal, they wouldn't be able to take on a second one. We're playing with that.

Other aspects of game balance boil down to small details that can only be sussed out after hours of play. "I've been thinking that the amount of [hit points restored] for the healing skill may not be that much. Then, talking to [Kosugi], I realized I may be a bad player," Salas explains, laughing. "So I'm rethinking that because other players could be more successful."

Kosugi is heavily involved in game balance as well. Right now, monsters chase players for a few tiles but give up as soon as players move outside of their field of view. When I called, he was in the middle of broadening their A.I. and is not sure how much more time he can afford to devote to the task given how little time remains in his 7-day period. Still, Kosugi takes it in stride, "I'm kind of hoping that if I prevent monsters from bunching up too much, especially near the players' initial positions, the randomness will just be part of the flavor of the game."

Grimm Bros. (Ash Monif, Randis Albion, Mark Domowicz)

Game: *Dungeon X: Flesh Wounds*
Date: Thursday, March 14th—Friday, March 15th

Domowicz is trying to stay calm. He is exhausted, lines of code are bleeding together, and their composer, Jade Leamcharaskul, has been too busy with other work to record sound effects for *Dungeon X*. To relax his nerves, he turns to a task under his immediate control: monster behavior.

While weak monsters can get away with ordinary attacks such as slashes and bites, the Grimm Bros. want to imbue certain monsters with special properties.

"I got a green slime in there, and he poisons you. That was easy to implement. We got the tree stump in there; he focuses on your pet and tries to kill your pet," Domowicz explains. As they descend deeper into the caves, players will have to adjust their strategy to counter poison and other special properties. Thanks to a bit of technical wizardry performed by Domowicz, players will be able to pan around levels in style.

> One thing I don't see a lot of in roguelikes is smooth camera movement. You'll often see roguelikes that have one or the other: you might see cameras that move smoothly from one tile to another, or the camera jumps along. In our engine, you'll have both.

Dungeon X: Flesh Wounds. Robin explores one of the cave environments (Image: Grimm Bros., LLC).

Albion and Domowicz have also implemented power-up items. The trio agrees that an inventory falls outside the scope of the 7DRL, so Albion and Domowicz created instant-use items. "In our game, maybe you pick up something and you do three times as much damage for the next 20 turns. Some items will deal some area-of-effect damage. Those are the kinds of items we'll implement for now," according to Monif.

Other than a nagging worry over the state of audio, Domowicz and the others sound tired but determined. They have 48 hours left on the clock, and one challenge remaining. "Take what we have and make it feel more like a game than a tech demo," Domowicz summarizes. "I think we've got everything else out of the way."

Ido Yehieli

Game: *Fisticuffsmanship*
Date: Wednesday, March 13th—Thursday, March 14th

Fisticuffsmanship is in good shape. Yehieli has streamlined the interface, added loads of weapons, and fixed the dungeon generator so it no longer creates unsolvable levels. The next and last step to achieving a certifiably finished 7DRL game is to add artificial intelligence.

"It's a generic A-Star algorithm," Yehieli responds when I ask him to explain how his A.I. will work.

> I have a bunch of code from previous games that I extracted from them and apply to different games. The AI in this game is not very smart; it's just trying to hunt the player. If it's distant from the player, it moves randomly. If you get close enough, it tries to path-find its way to you.

A-star is a longstanding A.I. algorithm in the games industry. The general idea is for all computer-controlled characters to calculate the shortest path to the player and take it, threading around obstacles as they go.

Yehieli chose the A-star algorithm because he has used it before, and because it works best for what he wants to accomplish. To counter the stream of foes heading toward them, players will have to think hard about how to move during their turns: move into a corridor and fight enemies one at a time, receiving a boost to defense for standing their ground; or play keep-away and wait for weapons like the hammer to charge up so they can deal as much damage as possible with every hit.

Although *Fisticuffsmanship* is finished, Yehieli believes some areas could be improved before the challenge's deadline. His calendar for day six looks full, so he will save the rest of the work for Friday, which "mostly involves adding features," he says.

> I want to add more enemies; I want to spawn weapons, because I have all sorts, but they're not really spawning in meaningful ways down in the dungeons; and I want to create more differences in the levels, perhaps by adding crates that you can smash and find stuff inside.

> *[Author's Note: Yehieli ended up feeling too*
> *tired after work on day six to talk.]*

Joseph Bradshaw

Game: *KlingonRL*

Date: Thursday, March 14th—Friday, March 15th

It happens to the best game designers: too much tinkering and bugs are bound to crop up. The particular roach that has Bradshaw tearing up *KlingonRL*'s virtual floorboards has been present since day one. "It happens one in a hundred times upon exiting [a star] system. With my luck, someone will be playing and they'll blow their game because of that."

The scenario in question crashes the game and all because Bradshaw tried to return to the sector map. Baffled for the time being, Bradshaw opts to work around the bug. To discourage players from acting recklessly, he wrote a condition where destroying a merchant vessel causes every ship in the player's current star system to go hostile. Players still have a chance to escape unscathed. Attacking removes their cloak, but if they stay alive for a few turns, the cloak renews, leaving their would-be assailants floundering.

Bradshaw reminds me that the player's ship will be cloaked by default. "When [enemies are] patrolling, they could bump you accidentally because they can't see you. If you get de-cloaked, they can see you, and they'll run after you." In addition to hostile Federation ships, the world will be populated by neutral vessels, which often contain valuable materials. These ships will flee when players become visible.

Crafty players might presume to get one over on Bradshaw. Lest players think they can win by heading straight for the Genesis device without stirring up enemies along the way, he will ensure they lack the fuel to make the whole round trip in a single attempt. Exploring star systems to stock up on fuel and weapons is a must. For him—and, he hopes, for his players—*KlingonRL* is about the journey, not the destination.

"I don't think I'm into playing roguelikes as much as I'm into the mechanics and the discussion of design," Bradshaw admits to me.

> As an attorney—or maybe it's why I became an attorney—the interplay of rules and the way things interact have always fascinated me. When I make my own games, by the time I've designed a system, the fun is over for me. I have no real desire any of the card and board games I've made. For me, [the fun is] designing the world.

When our conversation comes to an end, Bradshaw crawls back inside his code, determined to root out his bug.

7

Day Six: Tough Calls

Darren Grey

Game: *Mosaic*

Date: Friday, March 15th—Saturday, March 16th

"Today wasn't great," Grey says less than 5 seconds into our check-in.

When I left Grey the previous evening, he planned to finish writing the code necessary for monsters to move around. That kept him busy until 4:00 A.M. "It took a while to code different behavior patterns for each, trying to get all the numbers right and balanced, tweaking their colors so they stand out and suit color-blind people—things like that."

With the code in place, Grey stepped into the game to put his A.I. through a field test. Not all of it worked, but that was fine. Most code falls flat the first time out, but Grey was able to patch up most of the problems quickly. Other bugs had no easy fixes. In fact, some had no fixes at all. Two of the enemies inexplicably got stuck in corners. Each time, without fail, they moved to corners of the screen and huddled there, trivializing their defeat.

> It's quite hard to come up with an elegant solution to get out of that, because the whole idea was that they would have certain behavior patterns they would follow, and I wanted to follow them strictly so players could always predict how they would behave; I didn't want enemies randomly moving out of corners.

As of 6:00 A.M., Grey made the difficult decision to throw those two babies out with the bathwater. "That's annoying because I sunk a lot of time into

DOI: 10.1201/9781003196723-7

them, but the game is better off without them, quite simply. They're not worth trying to fix anymore."

Grey tries to look on the bright side. He nixed three enemies, but seven crafty foes remain. He figures he is out of time to implement a few fancy algorithms intended to show progression from level to level, but the tiles are varied and vibrant, and the button sequences he programmed in are fun to figure out and execute.

Unfortunately, Grey believes that even the bright side of his situation is gray and cloudy. After catching a few hours of sleep, he attended a party that he and his girlfriend had committed to months ago. Now he is back at his computer with 1 day left to finish *Mosaic*. The game is functional, and would qualify as a complete game in its current state. However, Grey worries that he has run out of time for *Mosaic* to reach its full potential.

> I've got less and less time now for a lot of the polish stuff I wanted, especially the sound design. It's looking like I might not have time to add in any of the sounds, which would be a shame. But I knew from the start that that might happen. The game will be complete in terms of the gameplay, and that's what really matters.

Before we disconnect, Grey goes over his plans for his next 24 hours: carry on tracking down bugs and getting *Mosaic* shipshape.

Bastien Gorissen

Game: *BattleRL*
Date: Friday, March 15th—Saturday, March 16th

Following our Skype call on day four, Gorissen pushed on. At lunch that same day, he was struck by a bolt of inspiration. A bug in the libtcod library where two keystrokes were sent to the game every time the user pressed a key once had inhibited his progress. To get around it, he needed to command the game to look out for extra keystrokes and remove them. His computer was not close at hand, so he grabbed the nearest piece of paper and jotted down the code he thought might do the trick.

Back at home, he typed in the commands he had scribbled down earlier and breathed a sigh of relief. They worked. It was a small victory, but after the stress of the workday, small victories were enough to boost his confidence.

Gorissen also found success implementing forbidden zones, areas that become closed off as the clock ticks down, forcing players into close proximity so they are forced to fight. He took the game for a test drive, saw the feature working as intended, and went to bed feeling happy.

On Thursday, his fifth day of work, his progress took a turn for the worst. "I'm pretty much swamped by work. I had to work very late and couldn't write a single line of code. I'm running a bit behind right now, but things happen."

Another screenshot from Gorissen's fourth day of work. Yu Narukami, one of the computer-controlled opponents (represented by the red "@" on the right-hand side of the screen), fails to flee a zone before it closes and becomes forbidden.

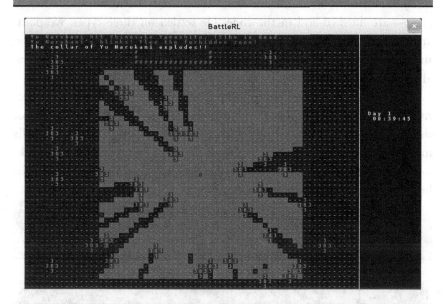

Gorissen awoke bright and early on day six, determined that he would not go down without a fight.

> Today is going pretty well, better than the last two days. I've mostly been working on finishing up the interface for the game. I added a minimap to tell the player where he is on the island, and to display the forbidden zones so you don't run into them unprepared.

As soon as he finishes the minimap, he moves on to designing a target interface that helps players aim ranged weapons like guns. When he is done with that, he will code up his menu and game-over screens. "It really does make a big difference in how you [perceive] the game: it goes from being a prototype or tech demo to a full game," he says in reference to the importance of glue screens.

Gorissen makes these plans under the assumption that he has enough energy left to finish. Another late night at work followed by another early morning left little time for sleep, much less the mental acuity he needs to make progress on *BattleRL*. His 7DRL challenge began at 2:00 P.M. on Sunday the 10th, leaving him just enough time for one last-ditch effort.

Edward Kolis

Game: *TriQuest*
Date: Thursday, March 14th—Friday, March 15th
By the time we meet for our chat, items—the last hurdle Kolis has to jump—are finished and in the code. He settled on three types: weapons, armor, and health potions. Health potions come in small and large varieties; small pots heal one member of the player's party, while large pots rejuvenate all three adventurers.

Tapping the 'w' or 'a' keys brings up the weapons or armor menu, respectively, where players can sort through their finds and equip gear that boost their favored stats. Players who build their party around the mage's spells might equip staves and armor that boost the mind stat, while players banking on the warrior's proclivity to hit first and ask questions later will favor heavy armor and big weapons.

TriQuest. The stats screen, placed above the minimap, allows players to keep an eye on their party's status.

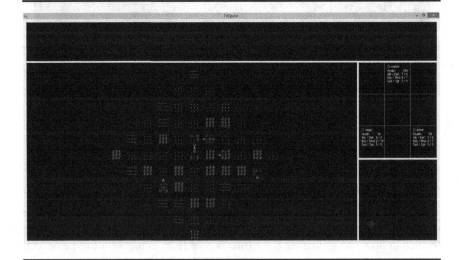

Kolis diversified weapons and armor even further by having them increase more than just attack or defense stats. For instance, certain weapons may inflict less damage, but they include a boost to body or mind, resulting in a net gain. While coding, Kolis overhauled the particulars of monster drops.

> I tried to make it so that none of the weapons or armor are significantly better or worse than any others, so I went away from the idea of monsters having specific [item] types they can drop. Instead, they have different categories: humanoids tend to drop weapons and armor, and animals drop potions because it would be silly for them to drop weapons and armor.

I mention that it sounds like *TriQuest* is in a state advanced enough to be submitted as a finished game. Kolis agrees and goes over the odds and ends he plans to polish off tomorrow,

> I'm thinking of implementing fog of war. If you walk over tiles, you can see them, but when you walk away, I want to show some terrain on the map so you can see what the area looked like. I also want some sort of ending sequence for when you win. I also need to write documentation on the controls and the game mechanics.

Joshua Day

Game: *Cogs of Cronus*
Date: Friday, March 15th—Saturday, March 16th

Once again, the titular cog-based puzzle system occupies a lower spot on Day's priority list than it warrants. Day agrees as much,

> My priorities have never been quite straight, but you do what you can when you can do it. I find that's the best way to optimize productivity. It's great to be able to work through things like a machine, but, honestly, if you don't have inspiration working for you, you just don't have time.

Perhaps to glean inspiration, or perhaps simply to cross off more tasks, Day spends the morning improving the game's infrastructure. He creates marble texture with swirling patterns that can be applied to walls, further diversifying caverns. Stairs sprout from the left or right edges of maps. Adding stairs required him to tinker with his dungeon algorithm, ensuring that rooms and floors connected properly. The message system displays messages properly, directly above the player, and banishes them as soon as the player presses a key or goes a short time without pressing a key.

Map boundaries have been firmly set.

> Up until now, it's been possible to move off the edge of the map.
> The game is designed with this system of cogs, so it doesn't really have a
> notion of boundaries of the map I corrected that and a few other over-
> sights in the process of getting those cogs ready to be interlocked and
> do what they're supposed to do.

Talk turns to the cog puzzles, and Day assures me that any puzzle that has to
do with moving cogs in the dungeons should work fine. He rattles off other
architecture-centric areas of dungeons he still wants to incorporate into the
puzzles. Lakes, for instance, and gases rising from floors and steaming from
walls, and maybe fire. "I've done fire so many times before that I'm tempted
to throw it in because it's easy and really cool."

Time is short, Day acknowledges as we bring our penultimate check-in to
a close. But he loves the pressure, especially when it emanates from a community waiting to play and pass judgment on their peers. He thrives on it.

> You get this sense of focus. You dive in and you work on a feature, and
> while you're working on it, you don't even think about how useful it's
> going to be; you just work, and work, and work, and you get it done.

Yuji Kosugi and Carles Salas

Game: *Versus Time*
Date: Friday, March 15th—Saturday, March 16th

Nearly all the ingredients have been added to Kosugi's and Salas's *Versus Time*.

> The next big task I'm going to work on is getting the [user interface] set
> up with the assets that [Salas] just sent me. Otherwise, we'll hopefully
> do some testing tomorrow to see what it's like to actually play the game.
> We'll possibly do some tweaks, maybe add more skills potentially.

I ask Kosugi if he has made a decision regarding movement: four directions
or eight. He decided that eight directions meant a minimum of eight keys per
player, which would take up too much space on the keyboard.

> I started thinking [about] two players, but I realized that as long as I
> kept the controls simple, I could scale up to three or four players. That's
> why I chose an interface that's just the four movement keys, plus two
> additional keys for the skill system.

Salas cracked his user interface (UI) problem from the previous day wide open.
To make the most efficient use of space on the screen, he will display each player's information in one corner. All in-game action will be displayed in the center

of the screen. Players can see how much life and time remained to them by monitoring how much red or blue remain in their life and time meters, respectively.

The UI also simplifies the process of keeping track of whose turn is up. As the active player moves, attacks, and invokes skills, the time meter slowly drains, going from blue to black. Once it's empty, the interface for the next player in line flashes, signaling that his or her turn has come up.

Both developers are enjoying the frenetic pace they have implemented. "I'm feeling great. I have problems concentrating when I'm not [working on the game] because I only want to do that," Salas says.

Salas still has a few ingredients to stir into *Versus Time.* He still needs to draw glue screens—menus, title cards, control layouts so players know how to perform in-game actions such as attacking and moving, and ending graphics that inform players whether they won or lost. "I think I can do that by the end of today, so tomorrow, I'll be able to focus on testing and tweaking."

"Testing and tweaking" summarizes how Kosugi plans to spend the next, and last, day of his 7DRL.

> We haven't tested it much as it's meant to be played, which is with multiple players. It's hard to tell what could happen under those circumstances. It could be that we'll get lucky and it's great already. Or, it might not be, in which case I'll have to think about what needs to change.

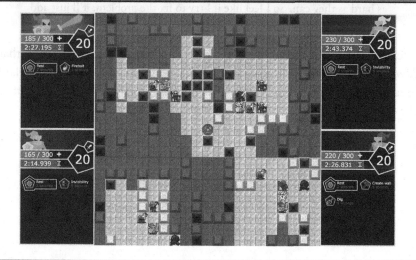

Versus Time. Each player's life (top red meter) and remaining time (bottom blue meter) is displayed in one corner of the screen. Other status info includes attack power and equipped skills, such as Rest and Invisibility.

Grimm Bros. (Ash Monif, Randis Albion, Mark Domowicz)

Game: *Dungeon X: Flesh Wounds*
Date: Friday, March 15th—Saturday, March 16th

Domowicz is at the end of his rope. "The code quality is on a slow decline. I'm pushing it in there as fast as possible just to get stuff done."

Even so, the efforts of the Grimm team are poised to pay off. A marriage of new code and artwork conceived a character generator that players use to name their avatar and adjust their attributes. Once the character generator is plugged in, *Dungeon X* can officially be declared a game.

"The guys who have been doing all the heavy lifting are [Domowicz] and [Albion]. Those guys are the rock stars," Monif lauds. *Dungeon X*'s producer extraordinaire has been collaborating with his IT staff for their game's grand unveiling. Clicking on the link Grimm Bros. will use to distribute the game whisks players away to the company website, where they must agree to a disclaimer before downloading the game files. There will also be a link to the company Facebook page so players can follow the game's journey from 7DRL entry to full-featured product.

Meanwhile, audio is still a problem to be solved. Monif took stock of his options.

> Sometimes when someone is behind, you have three choices: do nothing, do something, or cut the feature completely. At this point, I'm kind of doing nothing because everybody's already stressed out and working as hard as they can. So I feel like if I try to fix the problem, it'll just add more stress. Whatever gets in, gets in.

The guys have also been thinking more about pets. Monif explains that *Dungeon X* will pair each new player with a wolf, but they have already laid groundwork to offer a deeper experience in the finished product, still far off in the distance.

> You'll have to find them, and then you'll probably have to train them. We may even make it so that any monster can become a pet over time: a pet slime, a pet dragon—whatever you want. We have the code to support that; we just need to decide to do it, and do it.

Joseph Bradshaw

Game: *KlingonRL*
Date: Friday, March 15th—Saturday, March 16th

A bit of detective work led Bradshaw to the bug wreaking havoc in his game. It came as no surprise to him that *GameMaker* was the culprit. Behind the scenes, *GameMaker* appears to execute data and objects on the screen all at once. However, the simultaneous execution is just an illusion. *GameMaker* crunches calculations so quickly that it only appears as if all of them are being performed at once.

Bradshaw discovered that *GameMaker* gives priority to variables—which store game data—in a weird order. He ended up having to change the order in which he defined variables so that the player's ship's starting location was seen first. Once *GameMaker* knows where to find the player's ship, other data can be processed correctly.

Not that having to adhere to a fussy computer program's demands kept Bradshaw down for long.

> It's been a positive experience. It shows the amount of effort and work I can put in, and not run my body down. I'm not rundown at all. It's perfect. I get tired just because of the activity, but it does build my confidence.

Bradshaw has ample reason to feel confident. Over the 2012 7DRL, he developed *Sun Crusher*. It was, as he put it, "a blatant *Star Trek* rip-off." Players started with a ship that they could move a certain number of tiles per turn. To win, they had to guide their ship through a series of star systems until they reach the final boss, a Death Star fortress from *Star Wars*. "I hadn't stolen from George Lucas yet," Bradshaw explains with a chuckle. The infamous, moon-shaped battle station could only be destroyed with a sun crusher, a megaton missile capable of obliterating half the screen—including players, if their targeting was off.

Bradshaw loved the design of *Sun Crusher*, but the rest of the roguelike community didn't seem as keen on it. "I didn't do very well in the 7DRL judging because the game was only marginally like a roguelike game; there was no inventory management stuff unless you count your sun-crushing warheads, which most people didn't." Fortunately, Andrew Doull, another pillar of the community, thought highly of the game and ranked it fourth on the poll he ran on his blog, *ASCII Dreams*. "That was really exciting," Bradshaw remembers.

With any hope, he continues, even more people will latch on to *KlingonRL*, which he emphatically states is much more complex and interesting.

8

Day Seven: Verdicts

Darren Grey

Game: *Mosaic*

Date: Saturday, March 16th—Sunday, March 17th

Grey knew the jig was up. At the end of our conversation on Saturday evening, he looked at the clock and let reality sink in. He had approximately 19 hours left in the challenge—just enough time to finish writing last-minute A.I. routines and exterminate *Mosaic*'s few remaining bugs.

Gloomy over the fact that the game would not live up to the image of it he had painted in his mind, he goes through the motions. By the time he finishes tidying up, the clock chimes 1:00 A.M. Tired, but not ready for sleep, he picks up one of the pages he had torn out of *Mosaic*'s playbook.

> I was almost half-hearted at the start. I wasn't sure if I should bother putting sounds in at all, or just throw some basics sounds in. It was so late, and I hadn't had any sleep, and I could have just gone to bed. The game was pretty much done in terms of gameplay. But I thought, *I'll give this a go and see how this turns out.*

He takes a moment to consider how he wants to incorporate audio. Like Pachelbel's Canon in D, he wants to create a canon. With each move players take, notes from instruments should flow across the map—a few at first, then more as players move around and create colored tiles. To do that, he needs sound files. He opens his web browser and finds it surprisingly difficult to locate a pack of free sound effects that span an array of instruments, so he settles on piano keys.

DOI: 10.1201/9781003196723-8

The files come in an abnormal format, so Grey converts them to one that will work with his game. This process takes several steps. First, he has to convert them from their native format, .sf2, to an intermediary one, .sfv. Then he has to extract .wav files—one of the most common audio formats—from the .sfv files. Finally, the .wav files have to be broken down into a bite-sized format and loaded into *Mosaic*.

Once in the game, Grey moves his character around.

> When I finally got [the sounds] in, it worked. I had a plan for how to implement it, and I put that plan into effect. I called a sound every second or so to scan down a column [of colored tiles] and play notes according to what's in the column. Every second note, it would go down the next column, so it was getting called every second note.

Making music in the finished version of *Mosaic*.

At the first plunk of piano keys, his heart soars—and then drops into his stomach. Although the sounds work, they leave an unpleasant echo that detracts from the game's atmosphere. A few movements and the cacophony of notes and their echoes sound like a roomful of toddlers banging away at pianos.

Down but not yet out, Grey adjusts his plan. Pianos would not work, but another instrument might. Another pass through Google leads him to a package that contains audio files for every instrument in an orchestra. Even better, every instrument has been recorded playing notes in several tone ranges.

Grey feels his excitement growing, but knows he needs to start small. Before booking an entire orchestra to accentuate *Mosaic*'s mood, he needs to test a single instrument. He decides on the xylophone, an instrument known for producing shorter, clearer notes, which he hopes will circumvent the echo issue.

Indeed it does, but the result is just as grating on the ears. Grey is ready to give up, but the thought of failing to climb the heights he set out to scale leaves a bad taste in his mouth. He tries one more instrument, the harp. It sounds... better. Not great, but better. Good enough to convince him to stay the course.

> I looked at Pachelbel's Canon in D and how the music works. You've got a base instrument with a very deep sound going off every second or so. It varies slightly between the notes; it sticks within a certain range. Every four notes or so, a new instrument comes in. In looking at this and thinking about this, I thought about how I'd do something like that.

Instead of hitting on a brilliant new idea, Grey returns to one he had scribbled down before the start of the challenge. Instead of playing each note in a particular column of tiles, he assigns an instrument to each row but only activates instruments depending on the player's movements. His code will sweep across the map, checking each row to determine whether the instrument assigned to it should be active or inactive.

Working quickly, Grey assembles 11 instruments, including a cello, bass, flute, a viola, and a couple of violins. He also grabs a few note files for each instrument and writes code to raise or lower each note in pitch—for variety's sake, and to ensure that no instrument played so disparate a note that it sounds out of tune with the rest.

Grey writes his code carefully. He has no reason to rush. If this works, *Mosaic* will be a personal triumph, perhaps the best game he has written to date. If it does not—no big deal. The game can be turned in and declared a success by others, even if not by him.

At 6:00 A.M., Grey types in the last line, compiles the code, and runs the game. His "@" avatar appears, a treble clef threaded neatly through it. Grey runs his hands over the movement keys and sends his little character dancing over the map. A swell of notes floats from his speakers and lifts him from his chair.

> I cannot describe my reaction when I started the game up and started moving about, enabling the different squares so the notes started playing. It sounded fantastic. I jumped out of my chair and did a little dance of joy. It was actually quite hard to sit down and get back to coding.

Sleep is officially off the agenda. Grey recommences tweaking, giving the audio code a wide berth. It works. The last thing he needs is to muck it up. He complements the basic help file players can access in-game with a nitty-gritty document that goes into greater detail on move sequences and other options. Next, he assembles Mac and Linux versions to reach as wide an audience as possible.

Nearing the end of our time together, I ask Grey what his other testers think of the game. He admits that many players find it simple up until level seven when cleverer monsters show up, but that taking the easy way out filling in the entire map right away comes with a catch: once those players reach level seven, the difficulty is compounded by the fact that they had not taken the time to study enemies and learn move sequences designed to fill in lots of squares at once.

I mention that the musical notes tend to coalesce into an ominous soundtrack. Grey agrees and says that particular development is one he had not foreseen—he intended for the soundtrack to be soothing, like listening to classical music while playing a game of chess—but that his other testers found the tense atmosphere more to their liking.

"It took about five hours in total, from me sitting down to getting the music and getting it working in the game," he says, reflecting on the process of coding the audio.

> Which I think isn't too bad: only five hours of work for having not slept in 24 hours, and my mind shattered from the whole week, and having not done any [audio work] before in any capacity. Trying to do your own music generator as your first attempt to adding audio in a game is a big step, but it worked. It worked!

Bastien Gorissen

Game: *BattleRL*
Date: Saturday, March 16th—Sunday, March 17th
BattleRL is the first casualty among the projects I was fortunate enough to follow.

"It was pretty much a convergence of bad things," Gorissen admits when I ask what went wrong. "I had a lot of work during the week. That, plus the small amount of sleep I had because I stayed up late trying to complete the game, ended in me getting sick."

Just as detrimental as the blow to his health are under-the-hood computations that seemed promising earlier in the week.

> When I had 15 or 20 enemies [on the screen], the computation for move-ment was not as efficient as I thought it could be. You could make one move every 10 to 20 seconds, which is really slow for a roguelike game.

Growing ever more anxious as the hours wound down, Gorissen went into triage mode. He thought he might be able to submit a prototype, albeit bare-bones, if he could manage to corral all the bugs and speed up the glacial pace at which the game unfolded. Unfortunately, the tandem of sleep deprivation and a wicked cold made the mission insurmountable.

Gorissen chalks up his defeat to letting himself get absorbed in adding cosmetic details that should have been left for after he had completed the main game.

> For the first half of the week, I was like, 'Okay, I still have time. I can squeeze in hours here and there.' I should have used those two days [that I devoted to the challenge] to do more than just try to get the game to look pretty. I think that was a big mistake on my part.

Speaking candidly, Gorissen tells me he is gloomy over how his first 7DRL turned out. Still, he will not give up. There will be other 7DRLs to which he could carry the vital lessons he has learned. "I think most game devs have at least three games they really want to make at some point, and this is one is mine."

Edward Kolis

Game: *TriQuest*
Date: Friday, March 15th—Saturday, March 16th

When Kolis and I sync up for our final check-in, he confirms that *TriQuest* has been done for more than a day, leaving him plenty of time to buff out dents and scuffs. He typed up documentation to give players a quick-and-dirty overview of how to play, as well as describe the items, weapons, and monsters they would encounter. Amusingly, he has yet to find and kill the final boss, but he assures me the big bad lurks *somewhere* in the code, waiting for him to wander by.

> I know he's there because otherwise the game would tell me I won, and I haven't seen that. When you beat the final boss, you see a congratula-tions screen, and you get a choice between letting your heroes retire, or continue to wander around slaying the rest of the evil minions. If you kill the rest of the enemies, you get another congratulations screen. Just a little something for completionists.

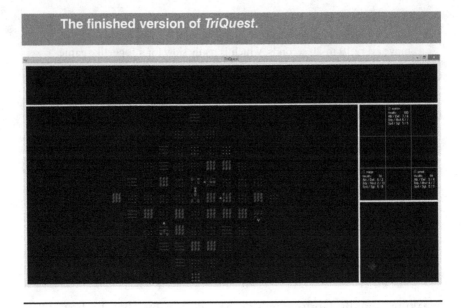

The finished version of *TriQuest*.

After crossing T's and dotting I's, Kolis added fog of war, a popular video-game mechanic that enables the minimap to show the ground that players have covered even when they're no longer in its vicinity. Fog of war allows players to easily distinguish where they have been versus where they still need to go. Black terrain on the minimap has yet to be discovered, while areas shrouded in the fog of war have been explored.

When I ask Kolis how *TriQuest* stacks up against his previous 7DRL games, he points to his new game as his best.

> I got a lot more done this time than I did in previous years. Either I got better as a programmer, or I just had more time because I'm unemployed. I think it's that I got better as a programmer, though, because I seem to recall being unemployed over the last two challenges I entered. [laughs] I'm glad to get this finished, and I hope folks like it.

Joshua Day

Game: *Cogs of Cronus*
Date: Saturday, March 16th—Sunday, March 17th
The sea of change that is Day's hectic week finally brings his ship to shore. Not dashed against the rocks, but not moored along the docks, either.

"The primary design goal, having cool puzzles in the game, totally failed to come to fruition. By which I mean I totally failed at that," Day says quietly. When he next speaks, I can tell he does so through a forced smile. "But I still have a success as a 7DRL, so I'm trying to focus on that."

Nothing went his way during the final 12-hour stretch. He turned in late the night before, planning to get 4 hours of rest and then return to the computer. His alarm spoke up right on the dot; exhausted, Day slept through it and lost 2 extra hours. He tries to convince himself that it had been for the best. He had been coding constantly and obviously needed the sleep.

In the early afternoon, he pushed his to-do list away and began implementing puzzles. It ended up being too little, too late.

> As I was adding [puzzles], there was something flawed in how I was detecting regions. I didn't have time to fix that. If I put in, say, boulders, every so often the algorithm would put a boulder in a place where you couldn't push it out of the way properly.

Hours slipped by. Finally, Day carefully considered the code on his screen. Without puzzles, he had a working game. With puzzles, he had a game that could not be solved. He made the choice to axe the cog-based puzzles.

> It was a really tough and painful call to make, but I decided that since I'm going to keep working on this game, I don't need to feel like the puzzles are the only thing is has going for it. For this version, having levels I can keep working on is by far the better choice.

Cogs of Cronus weighs in at six levels. Players can fight their way to the bottom and retrieve a MacGuffin, which triggers a victory message. Another 3 hours, Day tells me, and the game could be so much more. But he does not have 3 hours. He has, in fact, been procrastinating, putting off releasing the game in a desperate attempt to stuff in a few last features.

Day focuses on the positive. His dungeon generator has turned out swimmingly—better, in his opinion, than the one he wrote for *Rook*. He wrote over 1,000 lines of code on day seven alone, and knew it was necessary, perhaps even more so than the puzzle system.

> The huge majority was the stuff that was easy; it doesn't involve real decisions; it's just you-have-to-get-through-it code that handles inventory options rather than the inventory itself. Equipping, un-equipping, dropping—these things just have to be done. They take some time, they take some code, but they don't take a lot of fun.

Like other game authors through the years, Day simply bit off more than he could chew. He knew it, although he cannot be sure that adjusting his priorities earlier in the week would have worked out for the best. "I have mixed feelings about that strategy," he confesses, referring to the approach he had taken. "It worked out well. As I say, the decision to back off on having the puzzle generator killed me. But I had to make it."

Yuji Kosugi and Carles Salas

Game: *Versus Time*
Date: Saturday, March 16th—Sunday, March 17th

"We've finished up all the features and tried playing our game," Kosugi says as soon as our Skype call connects. Then, almost as an afterthought: "It was surprisingly fun."

Following yesterday's call, Kosugi and Salas tied all the various modules together. Kosugi took the colorful user interface (UI) Salas had painted and applied it to the game. To display numerals in the meters representing each player's health and time, he had to manually set the X and Y coordinates of where the numbers were supposed to appear on-screen. Until recently, the game assumed only two players would be playing, as only Kosugi and Salas were around to operate it. Now, up to four players can join in by pressing any of their assigned keys. Additionally, the final version drops players back at the main menu after they finish a session; older versions simply booted players back to the desktop.

Since placing each player's info in one of the screen's four corners had worked so well, Kosugi assigned keys based on corresponding locations on the keyboard. For instance, player one uses the WASD keys since they fall in the upper-left corner of the keyboard, and his or her stats likewise occupy the upper-left corner of the screen (more here give another key setting example to drive it home)

Like Kosugi, Salas expresses delight over how much fun *Versus Time* turned out to be.

> You can also play alone if you want. It's up to you: you may choose to go after another player, or wait for the monsters to eat the other players, or just try to survive depending on the position of the monsters. You can play the game several times and say, 'This time, I want to do this,' because depending on the players and the layout of the dungeon, you'll have to do different things.

Versus Time is up and running for players.

"Being competitive, the game is interesting because you're always looking over at the other players to see how strong they are," Kosugi adds. Like sharks following the scent of blood, players who notice that one of their opponents is low on health may choose to converge on him, then fight over the skills he drops.

Kosugi seems as proud of the development and design lessons he learned over the course of the challenge as he is over how *Versus Time* shook out. One lesson concerns a fundamental truth with which battle-scarred game developers can sympathize.

> I do know that this game is 6,000 lines of the worst code I've ever written because I've been under such a time crunch. I think, *Well, I really ought to rewrite this part and make it better, but I don't have time, so I'm just going to keep coding and make it even more of a mess.*

Above all, Kosugi feels vindicated.

> My thesis for making this game was that you could take a fairly traditional roguelike, make it multiplayer with a time limit, and that would be enough to make a competitive game. Based on the past couple hours of playing, that's proven to be true. I feel very good about that.

"We each had games we were working on, but this will be the first game we release," Salas gushes. "This is quite exciting. It's awesome. We were having so much fun."

Grimm Bros. (Ash Monif, Randis Albion, Mark Domowicz)

Game: *Dungeon X: Flesh Wounds*
Date: Saturday, March 16th—Sunday, March 17th

Dungeon X: Flesh Wounds (Image: Grimm Bros., LLC).

Donning his producer's cap, Monif made a call regarding the absentee sound effects. He knew about Jade Leamcharaskul's busy schedule when he brought her on board. Monif makes clear there was no bad blood between the crew and their new employee, but they agreed that *Dungeon X*'s gameplay and storybook-like graphics made for a fulfilling experience, and playing the game without any audial feedback would feel strange. The trio banded together and recorded as many sound effects as their remaining time allowed.

Now the team is finished and eagerly counting down the last 4 hours until midnight, when *Dungeon X* goes live. A link to the game will be posted on 7DRL.org, the official site of finished games for each challenge.

A few bugs still infest the code, but Domowicz foresees no difficulty tracking them down. "I think we're doing pretty well. We paced ourselves pretty well. We used these interviews to time our code updates. I think we're good. I'm feeling good."

Monif agrees, and once again directs all praise to his team. "We communicated well, we prioritized well, and the team has been working really hard. As soon as this is done, we're going to take a day or two to sleep."

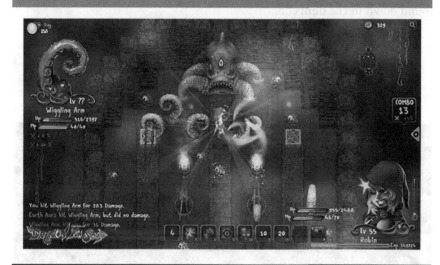

The team's primordial roguelike laid the groundwork for *Dragon Fin Soup*, released on popular gaming platforms in 2015.

Grimm Bros. does not expect to rest for long. According to Monif, a few days of much-needed rest will be followed by another round of polish on *Dungeon X* to get it ready for its first public appearance at the Game Developers Conference (GDC), which was scheduled to begin on March 25th. After that, the full team will come together and nail down details like the story. "We don't have a story yet," Monif admits.

> We have characters, we have a world, we have themes, and themes we're inspired by. Right now I'm actively taking point trying to come up with ideas. The team and I are going to review those ideas and try to solidify our story within the next day or two.

Before GDC and more meetings, though, Monif and the others will take time to bask in their 7DRL success. "This is kind of our first raw release that we're doing just for the roguelike community. To say, 'Hey, this was a blast, we had a lot of fun, so here you go.'"

Ido Yehieli

Game: *Fisticuffsmanship*
Date: Friday, March 15th—Saturday, March 16th

By the time Yehieli and I speak on day seven, *Fisticuffsmanship* is a wrap. All the weapons are present and functional, and Yehieli—who has taken the day off to finish up—was having fun testing all the unique attack patterns available to players through their movements as well as the weapons they found down in the dungeon.

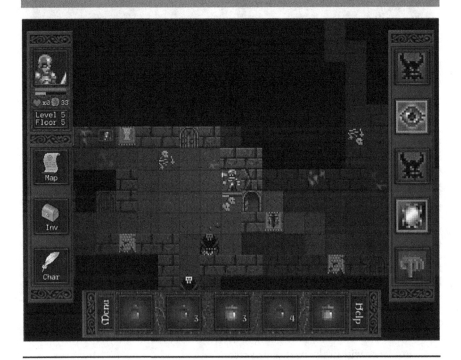

Yehieli designs roguelikes outside the annual 7DRL. Released in 2015, *Cardinal Quest* is one of his most successful ventures, netting him over $60,000.

Although he claims victory, Yehieli confesses that movement, the nucleus of his game, did not turn out the way he had hoped. Despite his best efforts, he feels dissatisfied with how confusing it can be to suss out how movement impacts gameplay.

> I can't really show those patterns. I'm telling you that you just created one after you moved, but that's hard to show. I felt from the get-go that it would be a bit obscure. But that's okay. I mostly wanted to see if it made sense on a basic level, and I'm willing to accept the fact that it's not a jump-right-in-and-play kind of game.

Still, Yehieli reasons, one of the joys of the 7DRL challenge is the opportunity to try something new. "I spent two full days and a couple of hours during evenings over the week. I'm happy I got to test out the idea, which I've had for a little while."

Joseph Bradshaw

Game: *KlingonRL*
Date: Saturday, March 16th—Sunday, March 17th

Bradshaw does not need Daylight Savings Time to get him out of a jam. "It's done and fun. It's as polished as it's going to get in a 7DRL."

I caught up with him in the middle of putting the finishing touches on his help file. Feeling less than satisfied with his messaging system, he wrote a help file explaining most of the game's mechanics and included accompanying screenshots to clarify portions that readers might not immediately comprehend.

Bradshaw reveals he is excited enough about *KlingonRL*'s potential to dive back in and tamper a little more once the challenge officially comes to a close. For the moment, he takes a well-deserved breather.

> This is like my coming-out party, like my sweet 16: I'm re-entering the world. I feel good about it. I have the energy, I have the brain power. I stayed up all night last night, got about four hours of sleep this morning, and I'm good to go.

Conclusion: When Dreams Meet Reality

In 2013, a record 350 contenders partook in the perennial 7-day roguelike challenge. Of those, only 155 were declared successful.[6] But the definition of success is fluid, even within the context of a 7DRL. Envisaging audacious and innovative features, and weaving them into your code with minutes to spare so that the game turns out more or less precisely as you imagined, as Darren Grey did, is one definition. Making the tough decision to cut one or more of those bold ideas so that you can turn in a game that is both functional and winnable, as Joshua Day did, is another.

American author Og Mandino eloquently summarizes a third definition of success, one that may seem counterintuitive at first glance: "Failure will never overtake me if my determination to succeed is strong enough." The very act of attempting an event as arduous as a game jam, which requires most competitors to balance real-world demands with their game-development aspirations, is commendable.

Bastien Gorissen continues to develop games through GSM Productions, the indie company he founded with friends in 2010. He has taken part in several game jams such as Ludlum Dare, where he and his teammates have successfully *completed several games.*[7]

Darren Grey remains active in the roguelike community. He participated in the 2014 and 2015 7DRL challenges, and emerged victorious both times. Equally as exciting for Grey, he has been able to flex his creative muscle in many other ways. He has written several short stories, some of which have been collected in anthologies, and writes for *Tales of Maj'Eyal* (*TOME*) and *Jupiter Hell*, both of which are roguelike games. You can read more about his projects, as well as his thoughts on roguelikes and game development, on his blog, "Games of Grey."

Edward Kolis remains as jovial and invested in gaming culture and development as ever. *Beware of Strange Warp Points*, his 2014 7DRL about exploring the vast reaches of space—an idea motivated in part by Joseph Bradshaw's *KlingonRL* game—was successful. He devotes much of his time to producing YouTube videos that deconstruct the designs of various indie games. You'll find him under the alias "Red Alien Gaming."

Joshua Day works on various roguelike games, including the popular *Brogue*, and occasionally pops by the Roguelike Radio podcast to co-host episodes.

Yuji Kosugi confided in me (half-jokingly, half-seriously) that his ultimate goal in designing *Versus Time* was to impress Darren Grey, one of his roguelike heroes. At Grey's annual post-7DRL meetup, to which Kosugi was invited, Kosugi got his wish, playing against Grey in *Versus Time* and leaving him duly impressed. Kosugi guest-hosted the *episode of Roguelike Radio* immediately following completion of the 2013 challenge and discusses the ups and downs of the week at length.

Carles Salas continues to dabble in game development, so long as those games do not include text-based graphics. He once again teamed up with Yuji Kosugi to create *Moonzooka*, a space shooter where players fought against gravity while firing moon bazookas at each other. The game was declared the winner of the 2015 *London Game Jam*.

Ash Monif, Randis Albion, Mark Domowicz, and the rest of the team at Grimm Bros. made good on their promise to continue evolving *Dungeon X: Flesh Wounds*. The game has since been renamed to *Dragon Fin Soup*, and is absolutely stunning in motion. Although they originally conceived the game for tablets like Apple's iPad, Grimm Bros. will be releasing *Dragon Fin Soup* in the summer of 2015 for Apple devices as well as PlayStation, consoles, and various PC operating systems including Windows, Mac OS X, and Linux. Check out new assets from the game, including videos, on the *Dragon Fin Soup* website.

Ido Yehieli is arguably as prolific in the roguelike community as Darren Grey. He is the developer of *Cardinal Quest* (one of this author's favorite roguelike games), which strips away many of the needless complexities of the genre and leaves players with a straightforward dungeon crawl that focuses on exploration and tactical combat. *Cardinal Quest*, its sequel, and myriad other games released by Yehieli can be found on *Tametick*, his website.

Joseph Bradshaw's climb from the depths of illness and depression culminated in a happy ending, which is no less than he deserves. He volunteered to serve on the panel of judges to award reviews and scores for the 155 successful 7DRL games submitted in 2013, alongside Joshua Day and Darren Grey. The judges needed several months to work their way through the games, playing each one long enough to gain an appreciation for its nuanced systems and themes. "Each of the following categories was graded from 1 to 3," the panel of judges explained on Roguelike Temple.[8] A higher number is better. Note that we reserved 3 for "truly excellent," so getting a 2 is a worthy accomplishment. The scores were spread across several categories such as completeness, aesthetics, fun, scope, and "roguelikeness." Bradshaw's game, *KlingonRL*, cleared a 2.56 average, the second highest score of the challenge.

Although not all of my roguelike friends succeeded according to the strictest sense of the world, their drive *to succeed* shows that failure is as valuable a teaching tool as victory. Roguelikes are notoriously difficult. Indeed, the genre's formidable reputation as the Mount Everest of gaming is what attracts players and developers to them in the first place.

Wise roguelike players do not pout, rage, or give up after their character perishes down in the dungeon, erased from their hard drive as if they never existed. They study the death, learn from it, and carry that knowledge into next year's quest.

Notes and Citations

1. I posted a notice on several popular roguelike forums: rec.games.roguelike. development (https://groups.google.com/forum/?fromgroups=#!topic/ rec.games.roguelike.development/1Nkdg6A33OM) and Rogue Temple http://forums.roguetemple.com/index.php?topic=3054.0.
2. *Broken Bottle* was my attempt to do what you may call 'games' as art: You can read more about *Broken Bottle*, Gruesome, and other "Games of Grey" on Darren's blog: http://www.gamesofgrey.com/blog/?p=124.
3. A veteran of the 7DRL challenge since 2008, he points to *Fuel*: You can play *Fuel* as well as other games made by Ido "Tametick" Yehieli on his website, www.tametick.com.
4. He devised a math-oriented game called *Decimation*: Check out Ed Kolis's games on his website, edkolis.exofire.net.
5. *Rook*, a game he created for a previous 7DRL: Download a copy of Joshua Day's *Rook* here: 7drl.org/2011/03/13/rook-7drl-success/.
6. Of those, only 155 were declared successful: "7DRL Challenge 2013." *Rogue Basin*. http://www.roguebasin.com/index.php?title=7DRL_ Challenge_2013.
7. He has taken part in several game jams such as Ludlum Dare: "About GSM Productions." *Ludlum Dare*. http://ludumdare.com/compo/ author/gsmproductions/.
8. Each of the following categories was graded from 1 to 3: "The 2013 7DRL Challenge Evaluation Process." *Rogue Temple*. http://www. roguetemple.com/7drl/2013/.

Index

Note: Page numbers followed by "n" denote endnotes.

Printed in the United States
by Baker & Taylor Publisher Services